Christian Faith in a Religiously Plural World

"CHRISTIAN FAITH IN A RELIGIOUSLY PLURAL WORLD"

Edited by Donald G. Dawe and John B. Carman

BR
127
.C47

ORBIS BOOKS
Maryknoll, New York 10545

Library of Congress Cataloging in Publication Data

Main entry under title:

Christian faith in a religiously plural world.

Sponsored by the Dept. of Religion, Washington and
Lee University and the Center for the Study of World
Religions, Harvard University.
    Includes bibliographical references.
    1. Christianity and other religions—Congresses.
2. Religion—Congresses. I. Dawe, Donald G.
II. Carman, John B. III. Washington and Lee
University, Lexington, Va. Dept. of Religion.
IV. Harvard University. Center for the Study of World
Religions.
BR127.C47   261.2   78-50927
ISBN 0-88344-083-0 pbk.

The Catholic Foreign Mission Society of America (Maryknoll) recruits and
trains people for overseas missionary service. Through Orbis Books Maryknoll
aims to foster the international dialogue that is essential to mission. The books
published, however, reflect the opinions of their authors and are not meant to
represent the official position of the Society.

CONTENTS

Preface, *by David W. Sprunt*   vii

Introduction, *by Minor Lee Rogers*   1

PART ONE
THE DIALOGUE WITH OTHER RELIGIONS

1. Christian Faith in a Religiously Plural World,
   by Donald G. Dawe   13
2. A Buddhist Response: Religion Beyond Ideology and
   Power, *by Mahinda Palihawadana*   34
3. A Hindu Response: The Value of Religious Pluralism,
   by K. L. Seshagiri Rao   46
4. A Jewish Response: The Lure and Limits of Universalizing
   Our Faith, *by Eugene B. Borowitz*   59
5. A Muslim Response: Christian Particularity and the Faith
   of Islam, *by Fazlur Rahman*   69

PART TWO
THE DIALOGUE WITHIN CHRISTIANITY

6. Religion as a Problem for Christian Theology,
   by John B. Carman   83
7. Religion as a Problem for the Christian Mission,
   by Gerald H. Anderson   104
8. Religion and Revelation, *by Charles P. Price*   117
9. Defining Religion from Within,
   by David F. K. Steindl-Rast   123

PART THREE

A RESPONSE

10. An Historian of Faith Reflects on What We Are Doing
    Here, *by Wilfred Cantwell Smith*　139

PART FOUR

EXPLORATIONS

11. Accounting for the Hope That Is in Me,
    by Alfred C. Krass　155
12. Translational Theology: An Expression of Christian Faith
    in a Religiously Plural World, *by John Ross Carter*　168
13. Is There a Theravada Buddhist Idea of Grace?
    by Mahinda Palihawadana　181

Preface

Something more than coincidence lay behind the fact that this symposium, "Christian Faith in a Religiously Plural World," took place on the campus of Washington and Lee University, Lexington, Virginia, and that its major sessions were held in Lee Chapel. As the university's president, Robert E. R. Huntley, is accustomed to note at the annual baccalaureate service, "the university began in the study of a minister and the religious impulse has been a powerful influence on this campus."

That impulse received a particular and enduring focus with the arrival of the institution's eighth president, General Robert E. Lee, in 1865. In the midnight of his defeat, Lee came to Lexington as the herald of a new dawn for the South and for the entire nation. A man who never countenanced any expression of hatred or vengeance, he deliberately undertook to make war-scarred, almost non-existent, Washington College a place of healing for his country's deepest wounds. To that end, one of his first projects was the construction of the chapel which now bears his name. It symbolized both his personal faith and his hope for his nation. The nature of his faith has been succinctly stated by his noted biographer, Gamaliel Bradford: "We may conclude that the cardinal fact in Lee's life was God; . . . everywhere and always he had God in his heart."[1] His hope was nourished by a keen awareness that his college post offered him a unique opportunity to contribute to the reconstruction of the South, and equally important to him, to the spiritual reunification of the nation.

Lee Chapel thus became the focal point of a remarkable ministry of reconciliation: a place where sons of former enemies on the field of battle were invited to worship, to pray, to sing together, not simply as fellow students but as citizens of "one nation under God."

It was, therefore, by no means inappropriate when in that same chapel Christian thinkers and concerned scholars from other religious traditions gathered one spring day to wrestle with the pressing problem of reconciling the historic Christian doctrine of the universality of the Christian faith with what many now perceive to be the permanent religious pluralism of the world. The symposium out of which this book has come was held April 22–24, 1976. It was jointly sponsored by the Department of Religion, Washington and Lee University, and the Center for the Study of World Religions, Harvard University, under the auspices of the Howerton Fund. The Philip Fullerton Howerton Fund for Special Programs in the Department of Religion was established by Mrs. Philip Howerton in 1973 as a memorial to her late husband. In addition, generous support has been received from the Fund for the Study of the Great Religions of the World, Colgate University. I wish to express my thanks and those of all the participants for the resources that made the symposium possible.

DAVID W. SPRUNT,
Chairman, Department of
Religion, and Chaplain,
Washington and Lee University

NOTE

1. Gamaliel Bradford, *Lee the American* (Boston and New York: Houghton Mifflin, 1912), p. 246.

Introduction

*Minor Lee Rogers**

The time will soon be with us when a theologian who attempts to work out his position unaware that he does so as a member of a world society in which other theologians equally intelligent, equally devout, equally moral, are Hindus, Buddhists, Muslims, and unaware that his readers are likely perhaps to be Buddhists or to have Muslim husbands or Hindu colleagues—such a theologian is as out of date as is one who attempts to construct an intellectual position unaware that Aristotle has thought about the world or that existentialists have raised new orientations, or unaware that the earth is a minor planet in a galaxy that is vast only by terrestrial standards [From a lecture, "The Christian in a Religiously Plural World," by Wilfred Cantwell Smith, 1961].[1]

A TIME FOR REFLECTION

The time has indeed come for members of the Christian community to face the challenges—theological, intellectual, and moral—posed by their increasing awareness of the religious diversity of humankind. This conviction led to a proposal to organize a symposium on "Christian Faith in a Religiously Plural World," to be held at Washington and Lee University. The kind of sensitivity Wilfred Cantwell Smith, currently Professor of Religion at Dalhousie University, so prophetically showed in his lecture in 1961 had become an inescapable part of the awareness of the Christian community. In the course of the two years of preparation for the symposium, three facets of the theme emerged.

First, the choice of the theme reflects a decision by Chris-

---

*Assistant Professor of Religion, Washington and Lee University

tians to take up a specifically Christian problem: the search for fresh ways to express the universality of Christian faith in light of the increasing awareness of our religiously plural world. There was a recognition that the Christian community would be well served by offering an opportunity for Christian theologians to do some more "homework" in anticipation of further conversations with representatives of other religious traditions. Thus, an important part of the task of the symposium was for Christian thinkers to engage in "intra-religious dialogue" to complement and undergird the vigorous efforts being made at "inter-religious dialogue" in many other forums today.

Second, it became increasingly apparent that Christian theologians would be able to work at this task more effectively, more realistically, if they were to do their thinking and make their statements in the presence of representatives of other religious communities — Buddhist, Hindu, Jewish, and Muslim. It would be even more helpful to invite these representatives to make prepared statements in response to major addresses by two Christian theologians. Thus, it became clear that the active participation of people of faith from other religious communities would be beneficial, perhaps even necessary, for a serious consideration of the theme on the part of Christians.

Finally, those of us preparing for the symposium discovered that the more we worked with the theme, "Christian Faith in a Religiously Plural World," the more we were aware that we had been grasped by a probing, challenging problem to which there were no ready answers. Or rather we saw too much at stake to leave the matter to a wide variety of too ready, conflicting answers. The most general formulation of this problem is the relation of the universal to the particular. On the one hand, Christian faith is "universal": In Jesus Christ, God has spoken to all humankind in every time and place. On the other hand, Christian faith is "particular": Christianity is only one tradition in a world which is religiously plural, which always has been, and which gives every indication of remaining so. The Christian thinkers preparing the major addresses were aware of many subtle implications of this problem as they sought to state their positions as clearly as possible, not only for their fellow Christians representing quite diverse strands of their own tradition, but also for Jews, Hindus, Muslims, and Buddhists. At the final session of the symposium, Wilfred Cantwell Smith, reflecting on what the participants had been doing, was to refer to the Christian problem as "the dilemma of universality and particularity." He went on to note a variety of ways in which this dilemma has been perceived within the Christian community: the dilemma of loyalty to the truth as perceived through our own tradition and sensitivity to the truth in the lives of people of faith in other traditions; or the dilemma of theological imperatives pushing us in one direction and moral imperatives pushing us in the other.

Not all Christians will agree that we have a problem. For some, Christian faith, because it demands exclusive loyalty to Christ, by definition precludes any such problem. Not all Christians will see a dilemma or paradox that commands our attention. In spite of increasing global communication, for some the fact of living in a religiously plural world remains an abstraction. I suspect that many of us who do see a problem are able to identify a moment in our lives when we became so engaged. For each of us, this moment may be informed in quite different ways. For some, it was the compelling moral witness evidenced in the life of an active participant in another tradition. For others, it has been through the insight gained by study and reflection on the teachings of a different religious tradition. Still others see the challenge of religious pluralism for Christian faith through the spirituality of those who live amidst a plurality of religious traditions with grace and integrity.

The dilemma of universality and particularity became vital to me personally through a friend who lives in southern Japan. Stricken at age thirteen with osteomyelitis, an extremely painful disease of the bone marrow, his legs and arms covered with dozens of incisions made in an attempt to arrest the disease, he has been bed-ridden for over fifty years. Despite continual pain, he is cheerful most of the time. He is sensitive to the concerns of others and to the world around him. A person of powerful and contagious faith, he was baptized as a young man through the witness of his physician, who was a Christian. He possesses a New Testament worn thin with his repeated marking of key passages and notes; he receives Holy Communion frequently in his home. In turn, he ministers to all who seek him out as friend and counselor; he is a leader in movements active on behalf of the physically handicapped.

One day, he said that in moments of pain or fright, he cries out "Namu Amida Butsu" (O praise Amida Buddha); in a similar manner, a Christian might cry out spontaneously "O Lord, O Lord." He had been nurtured in a pious Buddhist home, where his parents expressed their devotion by repeating the phrase, "Namu Amida Butsu," even as some Christians chant "Lord, have mercy upon us" as part of their liturgies.

This witness presents a puzzling contradiction to the Christian theologian, despite the fact that this Japanese friend sees no problem himself. He is a Christian in the deepest sense of the word, yet in moments of extreme need he calls on the name of the Buddha, Amida, the compassionate Buddha in the western paradise who has vowed to save all sentient beings. Are we to say that his humanity is graced with Christlike love, humility, and the spirit of service to his neighbor and yet is uninformed by Buddhist compassion? Or, is it sufficient to note that his humanity is grounded in an absolute trust in the saving power of reality or truth, which he addresses as Amida Buddha, apart from the saving grace of God through Jesus Christ? There appears to be no glib answer. It is not entirely satisfactory to speak of him as both *a* Christian and *a* Buddhist; the nouns would appear to mutually exclude. Yet, if we shift to the adjectival forms, Christian and Buddhist, would it not appear that in some sense he is both Christian and Buddhist? Surely, there is a paradox here worth pondering.

A further example. Wilfred Cantwell Smith, a student of the history of Islam, has observed that for some fourteen centuries, two sharply distinct answers have been given to the question, "Is the Qur'an the Word of God?" The Muslim community has answered, "Yes." Muslims have been willing to die as well as live for that answer, and in the process they have created a civilization of extraordinary richness and vitality. The Christian community has answered the question, "No." In fact, the matter has seemed to be unworthy of serious consideration. A simple "Yes" or "No" may not be good enough in our present world. Is there not a possibility for an alternative answer?[2]

Conflicting statements of belief abound. Turn now to a conference that brought together religious thinkers and philosophers at the University of Birmingham, England, in 1970. An Indian participant said that he believed in the transmigration of souls. A western Christian participant said that he did not. What are we to make of these contradictory statements?[3]

Christians who are less familiar with the question of religious pluralism as raised in relation to Buddhists, Hindus, or Muslims might choose to reflect on the fact that the Jewish community has been sustained over the centuries by the conviction that the Messiah or the Messianic Age is yet to come, while the Christian church is founded on faith in the Messiah who has come, once and for all, in the person of Jesus Christ.

In whatever particular terms the problem is raised for us, we share in an impasse of thought, unable to move freely to one side or the other, or forward or backward. But the problem remains. How can we most fruitfully approach this host of questions? Again, let me draw on my own experience, this time out of my work as a teacher in the field of religious studies.

A "KOAN" FOR CHRISTIANS

For a teacher of courses that each year encompass the whole of human religious history, the occupational hazard is an obvious one: There is too much material to present in too short a time. It is an impossible task. More important, there is also an occupational blessing. Amidst such diversity of materials, there is an incredible richness of religious symbols; there is an opportunity for living a liturgical year that is global in scope.

It was during the month preceding the symposium that I had occasion to reread portions of Zenkei Shibayama's commentary on the *Mumonkan* for one of my classes. Shibayama was a twentieth-century Japanese Buddhist monk; Mumon was a thirteenth-century Chinese Buddhist monk. The *Mumonkan* is Mumon's collection of forty-eight *kōan* with his commentaries. The first koan in Mumon's collection is known as Master Jōshu's *mu*, a term sometimes translated "emptiness" or "nothingness": "A monk once asked Master Jōshu, 'Has a dog the Buddha's Nature or not?' Jōshu said, *'mu!'* " The sixteenth is a saying of Master Unmon: "Unmon said, 'Look! This world is vast and wide. Why do you put on your priest's robe at the sound of the bell?' "[4]

Not infrequently, koans have been misunderstood as either perversely anti-intellectual or conducive to exploitive antinomian behavior. As seen within the Buddhist tradition, however, they are the statements, "sayings" or "doings," of an ancient master that freely and creatively express the wisdom of an enlightened state of mind. They are questions concerned with spiritual or religious truth posed in such a way that they point others to that truth. The fact that they have been passed on from master to student over the centuries, first in an oral tradition and later in written collections in Chinese, Japanese, and now English, suggests that they have been effective in that task.

In the training of a Buddhist monk in the Rinzai branch of the Zen sect today, the student does *zazen*, or seated meditation, with a koan carefully selected by his teacher. The koan serves as an instrument for presenting the mind with a paradox, a seemingly self-contradictory or absurd statement, resisting any facile solution. We are told that the student, agonizing in an effort to conceive a "solution" to the koan at all costs, is led to an abyss of despair before being awakened to a new state of understanding of the human condition and the universe.

Some of us who participate in human religious history as Christians discovered in the symposium's theme of religious pluralism a "koan" for Christians. Like a koan, the problem of relating the particularity of Christian faith to its claim to universality is a paradox worthy of consideration. It is a moral, spiritual, and intellectual problem that is crucial for the continuing vitality of the Christian community. Like the koan this paradox admits of no simple or already evident solution. It calls for serious reflection to stretch, indeed to transcend existing lines of thought and even of belief, to encompass what has long remained unnoticed and unbridgeable. Finally, we would have to say that the koan for Christians may require sustained meditation to give us new light on how loyalty to Jesus Christ and his lordship is to be conceived in a religiously plural world.

Christian theology, of course, is not unfamiliar with paradox or, to use our term, "koan." Contemplatives within the Christian tradition have perceived the doctrine of the Trinity or the person of Christ as subjects for meditation. Their guidance would be a rich resource for those who choose to take on this Christian koan. At the same time, a decisive factor in helping us to identify the Christian problem may prove to be the contribution of representatives from the Buddhist, Hindu, Jewish, and Muslim communities, such as those who agreed to join with and work with Christian theologians at the symposium. In recognizing their contribution, we will have an opportunity to write a new chapter in the history of the Christian community together, a chapter that might come some day to be seen as one chapter in the religious history of all humanity.

It is noteworthy that each of the ten leaders invited to participate in the symposium—including a Jew, a Muslim, a Hindu, and a Buddhist, as well as Baptist, Catholic, Episcopalian, Methodist, Presbyterian, and United Church of Canada Christians—was willing, first, to accept the invitation, and second, to take up and become engaged in a Christian koan. Each of those invited agreed without exception to attend; a brief glance at their backgrounds offers possible clues as to why they may have come.

Donald G. Dawe, Professor of Systematic Theology at Union

Theological Seminary in Virginia, had returned recently from a journey to northern India and Nepal where he had an opportunity for conversations with members of the Tibetan Buddhist community in exile. He has worked extensively also with the Sikh community. He agreed to give a major address, "Christian Faith in a Religiously Plural World." Four scholars representing the Buddhist, Hindu, Jewish, and Muslim communities accepted invitations to respond to his address: *Mahinda Palihawadana*, Professor of Sanskrit, University of Sri Lanka, had made studies probing whether in Theravada Buddhist thought a notion comparable with "grace" in the Christian tradition is discernable; *K. L. Seshagiri Rao*, Professor of Religious Studies at the University of Virginia, had written a major study on Hindu-Christian dialogue focusing on Mahatma Gandhi and an Anglican Christian missionary, C. F. Andrews; *Eugene B. Borowitz* of Hebrew Union College-Jewish Institute of Religion, New York, had done significant work in Christian theology; and *Fazlur Rahman*, a Professor in the Department of Near Eastern Languages and Civilizations at the University of Chicago, formerly serving his native country, Pakistan, as Director of the Central Institute of Islamic Research, had written frequently on topics pertaining to Islam's role in the modern world. Each of the four is a scholar whose studies have related at some point to the Christian tradition. Each is an active participant in his own religious community and at the same time is in close touch with members of the Christian community.

John B. Carman, Professor of Comparative Religion and Director of the Center for the Study of World Religions at Harvard University, agreed to give the second major address, "Religion as a Problem for Christian Theology." Born in India of Christian missionary parents, he has had an abiding interest in the problems of Indian Christians in relation to Hindu culture. Three Christian theologians accepted an invitation to respond to his address. *Gerald H. Anderson*, Director of the Overseas Ministries Study Center, Ventnor, New Jersey, is a Christian missiologist devoted to a rethinking of the Christian missionary movement, a rethinking to be informed by the work of Christian theologians who are natives of Asia, Africa, and Latin America. *Charles P. Price*, a Professor of Systematic Theology at the Protestant Episcopal Theological Seminary in Virginia, had taught introductory courses in Christianity to members of other religious traditions and was preparing an introduction to Christianity for Muslims at the invitation of Muslims. *David F. K. Steindl-Rast*, a Benedictine monk and a native of Austria, had been engaged for many years in conversations with fellow monks who are Buddhists and Hindus. Again, each respondent is a scholar and at the same time is an active participant in the life of his own religious community. Each has lived among and worked with members of other religious traditions.

Wilfred Cantwell Smith was invited to make a final statement, "An Historian of Faith Reflects on What We Are Doing Here." Over a decade earlier, in the introduction to the series of radio talks published as *The Faith of Other Men*, he had witnessed to the importance of his own experience of living and of teaching in a Christian College in Lahore, where his colleagues were people of faith—some Christians, some Hindus, some Muslims, and some Sikhs. At about the same time, it was he who had posed the koan, unwittingly or not, with which we were now struggling. Seeing that his colleagues were responding to issues that he had raised, how could he refuse our invitation?

In sum, then, the speakers at the symposium participate in and thereby represent a plurality of religious traditions; others who chose to attend testify to their recognition of the relevance of the issues raised for Christians living in a religiously plural world. The symposium's theme, "Christian Faith in a Religiously Plural World," addresses a Christian problem. Both those who are Christians and those who are not appear to have recognized a human problem.

NOTES

1. Wilfred Cantwell Smith, *The Faith of Other Men* (New York: Harper and Row Publishers, Inc., 1972), p. 123.

2. See Wilfred Cantwell Smith, *Questions of Religious Truth* (New York: Charles Scribner's Sons, 1967), pp. 39–62.

3. See Wilfred Cantwell Smith, "Conflicting Truth-Claims: A Rejoinder," in John Hick, ed., *Truth and Dialogue in World Religions: Conflicting Truth-Claims* (Philadelphia: Westminster Press, 1974), p. 161.

4. The discussion of the concept of koan presented here is largely informed by two writers: first, Zenkei Shibayama, a former master of a major Zen temple in Kyoto concerned that his own tradition be made available to people in the West; and second, Carmen Blacker, Lecturer in Japanese at Cambridge University, concerned that members of her own Christian tradition learn from Buddhists. See Zenkei Shibayama, *Zen Comments on the Mumonkan* (New York: Harper & Row Publishers, Inc., 1974), and Carmen Blacker, "Methods of Yoga in Japanese Buddhism," Strong Trust Lecture for 1968, in *Milla wa-Milla*, 8:31–46 (1968).

PART ONE

THE DIALOGUE
WITH OTHER RELIGIONS

1

Christian Faith in a Religiously Plural World

Donald G. Dawe

In a seminar at the Harvard Center for the Study of World Religions some years ago, Dean Krister Stendahl of the Divinity School suggested an analogy to the contemporary religious situation from the realm of nuclear energy. He suggested that our problem in religion is similar to that of the scientists searching for ways to release the potential of nuclear energy. The problem with nuclear energy is to find ways to release the tremendous power of the atom without the danger of the deadly fallout of radioactive wastes. In religion, Dean Stendahl suggested, the problem is one of releasing the great power of human faith and devotion without the deadly fallout of destructive hatred and mutual animosities they have so often produced.

Religion is a basic means of human identification and community that has marked off, as well as bound together, human beings. Its paradox is the ways in which the depth and constancy of love for those within the community of faith has often been denied by the hatred and contempt for those outside that community. The power of religion has been released so often at the price of the terrible fallout of human suffering visited upon others in the name of religion. This is a price humankind is no longer willing or able to pay.

It is particularly significant that Dean Stendahl, speaking as a Christian in a religiously plural community of scholars, should voice this concern. For he was enunciating a concern that is ever more pressing on the hearts and minds of Christians. Christianity is a religion that combines the claim to being universal in scope with the demand for being exclusive in belief. Confessional statements from the earliest strata of its history reflect this universalism. "Jesus Christ is Lord of all." He is the Savior of all people who has been sent by God. His disciples became apostles commissioned to "go therefore and make disciples of all nations . . . " (Matt. 28:19). At the same time, Christians confess that Jesus Christ is the only Savior. "And there is salvation in no one else, for there is no other name under heaven given among men by which we must be saved" (Acts 4:12). Spiritually and intellectually the root problem is one of finding new ways for the Christian community to relate the particularity and universality of its faith. This symposium is part of the struggle to make sense out of Christian faith in a religiously plural world.

Throughout its history, Christianity has displayed with blinding intensity the contrast between love and aggression, sacrifice and hatred. How is release to be found from the destructiveness associated with this religion, while still keeping open its power to enlarge and enhance human life? This question has pressed upon us with ever greater intensity in the twentieth century, when the search for world community has become an insistent priority. Christians have become aware of not only physical violence but also the emotional and spiritual violence associated with its particularity. Historically this violence has been aimed not only at other communities of faith, as in the Crusades, but it has also been turned against ourselves, as in the Inquisition or the wars of religion between Christians.

Two events of the twentieth century have brought to focus with inescapable clarity for the Christian community the implications of the ways in which it has interpreted its particularity and its universalism. The first is the Holocaust, where the terrifying implications of anti-Semitism became evident to the Christian community and has compelled a deep, and as yet, incomplete reappropriation of its faith and the definition of its community. The second is the encounter with the non-Christian religious traditions of the world by western Christendom.

The colonial expansion of the countries of western Christendom into the rest of the world from the sixteenth through the early twentieth centuries was accompanied by a missionary movement that put Christian faith into contact with Hinduism, Buddhism, Islam, Shinto, Tao, and the tribal religions of the world. Initially, this contact was viewed as the occasion for the replacement of these religions by Christianity. It was predicted that the universality of Christianity would be actualized by the conversion of all people to its particular faith. At this point in the twentieth century, we know this is not to be the case. If I may use a word picture from the Bible, Christians sounded "the Gospel trumpet," but unlike the case of Joshua of old, the walls of the city of the unbelievers did not come tumbling down. The "Jerichos" of the other religions did not collapse in inner contradiction or seek their salvation in becoming Christian. In fact, today, we live in the midst of a small, but highly visible, reverse missionary movement in which non-Christian forms of spirituality are appealing to those for whom the culture religion of western Christendom has broken down. This means that any rethinking of the universality of Christian faith has to take as its starting point the incurable religious pluralism of the world. The world has always been religiously plural, and it gives every evidence of remaining that way. Any vision of the universality of the lordship of Jesus Christ has to take this fact seriously. Hence, the title of this paper and the subject of this symposium contain already the foundation assertion for interpreting the universal claims of any particular religious community. All claims to universality have to be related to the fact that no particular religion will be the sole religion of humankind.

I

The rethinking of the relationship of Christianity to other religions must proceed from within and not without Christian faith and tradition. In finding a new way in which to relate the particularity of the Christian religion to its claims of universality, one thing is excluded. It cannot be done on a basis that is unintelligible to Christians nor on a basis that distorts the other religious traditions to which it is being related. Ignoring this limitation has been the hidden problem in the modern search for dialogue between religions. The modern concern for dialogue between religions has proceeded, on the side of western civilization, at least, on the basis of the rationalistic humanism of the Renaissance and Enlightenment. The rise of modern secularity has provided Christianity a means for building bridges to other religions on the basis of a new understanding of ultimate reality that proceeds from human reason. Some philosophical conception of the Absolute or universal vision of human nature was to provide the basis for overcoming the demonic forms of particularism that had characterized the relations of Christianity to other religions. An honorable succession from Edward Lord Cherbury, in the seventeenth century, to William Hocking, in the twentieth, has stood in this tradition.

The difficulties with such a basis for dialogue between Christianity and other religions have become evident. Not only has critical philosophy rendered its intellectual foundations obsolete, but the philosophical doctrines of this tradition distorted both Christianity and the religions to which it was seeking to relate. While motivated by evident goodwill, the modern dialogue of religions has proceeded at the price of remaking every religion over into a version of philosophical monism or rationalistic humanism.

Modern secularity has offered another way of dealing with religious pluralism. As religious traditions lose their importance as means of self-understanding and community identification, their differences and mutual exclusiveness diminish in importance. Alienation from any particular religious faith tends to move the question of religious particularity into the realm of indifference as life is determined by nonreligious values and institutions. Yet secularity has been no more successful in establishing human community than has the religious vision. The competing claims of nationalism, economic imperialism, and ideological triumphalism are also demonic forms of particularity that have not been able to establish a new universality in human community. Neither the secular ideologies nor religious visions can claim to be the unique source of a universal human community. Rather they are both caught in the ambiguity of a demonic particularism that distorts all claims to universality. So the fact remains that the religious question has to be dealt with in the religious perspective. The problem of Christian faith in a religiously plural world cannot be solved by ex-Christians learning to relate to ex-Jews, ex-Buddhists, ex-Muslims, or ex-anything else, in the name of conceptions that do not take these traditions seriously.

The advent of modern secularity has forced upon the religious communities the need for a radical honesty about themselves and their claims. For Christians this means that either they give up their claim to universality, or it has to be substantiated by some new vision that shows the reasonableness of its claims. If there is no basis within the Christian tradition other than that of Christian triumphalism, in which all other religions are to be replaced, then the only possibility is to move outside the tradition to find a new basis for relating to others. The thesis of this paper is that such a move is unnecessary. There are possibilities within Christianity that both legitimately express the meaning of its revelatory events and allow it to be related in new, nontriumphalist ways to other religions. In order to explore these possibilities, it is necessary first to engage in a kind of "in-house" reflection on the origins and traditions of Christianity.

II

At the heart of Christian faith and at the source of its traditions in Scripture is the belief in a covenant. Covenant is one of the basic categories by which ancient Israel and the early church interpreted the revelatory events that constituted their life and faith. The concept of covenant has remained a structural element in Christian thought ever since. For this reason, the investigation of the covenant concept can provide a key for rethinking the relationship of the particularity of Christianity to its claims to universality.

A covenant is a promise or agreement between two parties, solemnized by an oath, that binds the parties to it to fulfill the promises they have made. There are a number of covenants reported in the Bible. In these, God enters into a special relationship with various people or communities. The two most prominent of these covenants in Christian theology are the one made with Abraham that establishes the Hebrew people in their special relationship with God (Gen. 15 and 17:1–14) and the covenant made in Jesus that is said to constitute the church (Matt. 26:28, Mark 14:24, Luke 22:20, and 1 Cor. 11:25).[1] But these are by no means the only covenants. For covenant is a conception that extends for biblical religion from the divine creation of the world to its hoped for consummation by God. The covenants were not simply the means for securing the particularity of certain communities but also the means for expressing the universality of God's sovereignty. However, to understand this it is necessary to determine with whom God has entered into covenant, and what is the purpose of the different covenants. Two very different sets of answers to these questions are possible. The first is that of traditional Christian triumphalism.

The covenant theology of Christian triumphalism, while open to many variations, may be stated fairly simply. The foundation is laid in the Old Testament when God called through Abraham a particular people for himself. He promised to be "their God" and they pledged to be "his people." From the special character of this relationship, it was deduced that ancient Israel, as the People of God, were the saved and the rest of humankind damned. While Jewish exegetes were slow to reach this conclusion, Christian interpreters were not. Calvin could speak of the ancient Hebrews as the church under the old covenant. The nations of the world did not know the Law nor the "one, true living God" of the Hebrews. They stood outside of the redemptive purposes of God.

When the Christian church took over the Jewish Scriptures as part of its own canon, it applied the separatism of ancient Israel as a characterization of its own relationship to the world. However, the Christians then gave this covenant theology a new twist to heighten its particularism. They expelled the Jews from the covenant relationship to God and put themselves in their place. The argument was that a "new covenant" had been established through Jesus Christ that superseded the old one in Abraham and Moses. The church alone was now the holy people of God, the saved amidst the damned. The church is the covenanted people of God and can provide the only means of salvation. By the time of Cyprian (d. 258), this theology was established as the basis for interpreting all the covenant traditions of the Bible.[2] It was summed up in the dictum, "Outside the church no salvation."

While such a reading of the covenant theology is an evident part of Christian tradition, does it accurately interpret the revelatory events of Christian faith or their basic biblical formulation? The answer is clearly "no." In the first place, such an interpretation overlooks the setting given for the call of a special people through Abraham, and it also distorts the task for which the special people is elected. The purpose of calling a special people by God is not for their salvation and everyone else's damnation, but for their establishment as a witness people to God so that through them "all families of the earth will bless themselves" (Gen. 12:3).

The context for the call of Abraham is the prior covenanting action of God reaching back through Noah to Adam. There is an older pre-Abramic covenant that God had made with the whole of humankind. The special covenant made through Abraham has its setting within the larger universal covenant made through Noah by which God has entered into a covenanted relationship of care with all humanity.

The legends of the call of Abraham and the giving of a covenant through him (Gen. 12–17) find their setting in the Bible in the context of a mythical, primal history that reaches back to the creation of the world (Gen. 1–11). The election of Abraham and through him Israel has as its setting the universal election of all people through Noah. The Hebrew flood story, with its evident roots in the Gilgamish Epic, becomes a myth of divine judgment and new creation in the book of Genesis. Noah, the just one, is saved along with his family from the flood to be the basis for a new beginning in which God pledges his fidelity to all creation. After the flood, God establishes a covenant through Noah with "every living creature of all flesh" (Gen. 9:15) in which he promises never again to destroy the world in judgment. He also promises to provide the seasons, and he gives dominion over creation to human-kind as its underlord. The covenant is sealed by the rainbow, the symbol of God's abiding promise.

The imagery of the rainbow in the Hebrew text is important. God calls the rainbow "my bow in the cloud" (Gen. 9:13). The Hebrew term for the "rainbow" is elsewhere in the Old Testament used to characterize the "bow of war."[3] God shows the world in the rainbow that he has put aside his bow. He will never again loose his "bow of war" against the whole world and reduce it to chaos.

The crucial thing to remember is that the covenant in Noah is not conditional upon the response of men and women to it. It is clearly recognized that human beings are sinners and will remain such, a fact that Noah and his sons abundantly prove right after the flood. The covenant is made on the initiative of God and is sustained by God's faithfulness, despite human sin. This covenant reaches through Noah not only to "every living creature" but also to "all future generations." As such, Jean Daniélou has called it "the cosmic covenant."[4]

There is still another tradition that sees the act of creation itself as a covenant between God and all humankind represented in the primal couple, Adam and Eve. Ben Sirach, in a second century B.C. reflection on the creation narratives, says of Adam and Eve: "He made an everlasting covenant with them" (Eccles. 17:10). As this commentary makes clear, the primal history asserts the commitment of God to all humankind as summed up in Adam and Eve. It is the larger context that gives the special covenants formed later their meaning and purpose. These later covenants, with the Hebrew people and the church, are covenants of disclosure in which God reveals his nature or name. The covenanted people are given the name of God that they may share it with others, so that all the nations "shall bless themselves."

In the covenant of disclosure the divine name is made known first through Moses and then through Jesus Christ (Exod. 3:13–15, Phil. 2:9–11). To know the name of God is not simply to have a bit of esoteric information; it is to know the pattern of God's redemptive presence in the world. To know the name of God is to know how he will work in judgment and redemption in all human history. This disclosure, given in and through the people of the special covenant, Israel and the church, points to a scope of activity that embraces the whole world. The critical reflection on the life of the covenanted people by the Hebrew prophets makes this clear. According to the prophet Amos, just as the ancient Hebrews had been saved by God from Egyptian bondage, so God also brought the Philistines from Caphtor and the Syrians from Kir. Israel is the chosen of God, yet at the same time, Yahweh declares through the prophet, "Are you not like the Ethiopians to me, O people of Israel?" (Amos 9:7). The turning of the Chosen People from the law of God, for which they are set as an examplar, is greater, according to the prophets, than the forsaking of the law by other nations. Ezekiel admonishes Jerusalem that "she has wickedly rebelled against my ordinances more than the nations" (Ezek. 5:6). He chides his people with the fact that other nations have a knowledge of the law to which they are more faithful than is the Chosen People.

The covenant is one of responsibility, not privilege. The special quality of the people in the covenant of disclosure is set by their summons to witness to the full scope of God's presence and work. It is this call to witness and their failure to fulfill it that brings the people in the covenant of disclosure under judgment. They are not free of judgment, while other people receive judgment. Instead, paradoxically, they receive "from the Lord's hand double for all her sins" (Isa. 40:2). When they are saved it is to allow them to carry on their work of witness to God (Isa. 55:5).

Theologically viewed the basis for these covenant traditions is what Richard Niebuhr called "radical monotheism."[5] The conception of ultimate reality has been ridded of the vestigial remains of the tribalism that locates God in one place or allows people to move away from God's presence (Gen. 4:16, cf. Ps. 139:7–11). But radical monotheism is more than the rejection of localism, it is also the rejection of a false particularism. The logic of monotheism can be given a perverse turn. Monotheism can breed a particularism that argues that since there is only one God, wherever he is not known and honored by his particular cultic name, there is only damnation and darkness. By contrast, radical monotheism proceeds from belief in one God who is Lord of all. It gives a very different vision of the world. This vision is seen in the prophet Malachi: "For from the rising of the sun to its setting my name is great among the nations, and in every place incense is offered to my name, and a pure offering; for my name is great among the nations, says the Lord of Hosts" (Mal. 1:11). Starting from faith in one God, Malachi is able to see the honest worship of all the nations being offered to the Lord. In the vision of radical monotheism, the particularism of the covenanted people is not ignored but transformed. It is not the particularism of the saved against the damned but the particularism of a people that has been given a vision of God by which the world may be illumined (Isa. 49:6). Their particularity is the means by which the universality of God is to be acknowledged.

III

The question of particularity and universality becomes most acute in the New Testament, where the covenant of disclosure becomes focused in one person, Jesus of Nazareth. No longer is the focal point of revelation a nation and its relations with other nations. Revelation is in the life of a particular man who lived in first-century Palestine. His words, his acts, and, especially, the circumstances surrounding his death are remembered and valued as disclosures of God. This is seen in the ways in which Jesus is characterized in Christian tradition. He is spoken of in the most exalted and universal terms. He is confessed as Lord, the embodiment of the divine Logos that has created and now sustains the world (John 1:1–3). Through his earthly ministry, death, and subsequent resurrection-exaltation, a cosmic drama has been initiated. The demonic powers are being overthrown and the kingdom of God is being established. While the final victory of the kingdom is not fully evident in history, the time is confidently awaited when God shall be "all in all" (1 Cor. 15:28). This ultimate triumph of God's rule of righteousness in the world was characterized by the term "new covenant" (1 Cor. 11:25, Heb. 8:13 and 12:24). It was a covenant that was ratified by the death and resurrection of Jesus. However, in its fulfillment it points to the future.

In speaking of a "new covenant" Jesus and the early church were reflecting on a tradition that goes back to earlier Jewish prophetism (Jer. 31:31–34). The new covenant is eschatological. In its full actuality, it lies in the future. It is the covenant of the kingdom of God in which all nature and humankind will be transformed. Prophets had looked forward to this kingdom. Jesus in his death had ratified this new covenant of the kingdom. His life, death, and resurrection were the seal or assurance of the promise of the kingdom's coming. The Spirit of the Risen Christ is now the assurance to the faithful that the kingdom will come. But the focus of the new covenant is the kingdom of God that still lies in the future.

The old covenant is dependent upon religious institutions, cultic acts, laws, and teaching for its expression and maintenance. This old outward covenant is becoming obsolete. In the new covenant, knowledge of God and his law will be immediate and direct. Yet as long as humankind lives within history, the particular outward institutions and teachings of the church will be needed as the means for calling people to respond to the presence and activity of God. Commenting on the prophetic promise of the new covenant, the Epistle to the Hebrews says: "In speaking of a new covenant he [Jeremiah] treats the first as obsolete. And what is becoming obsolete and growing old is ready to vanish away" (Heb. 8:13). The old covenant has been overcome in principle. But it has not yet passed away and will not until the end of history.

The idea of a new covenant has posed difficult interpretative problems for Christian theology. The question of the meaning and locus of the new covenant in time and place is determinative for how Christianity is to be related to other religions. The tradition of Christian triumphalism has taught that this new covenant replaced the old covenant made through Abraham and Moses. The Jews have been replaced as the covenanted people by the church. The roots of Christian anti-Semitism were laid in this doctrine of supercession or replacement that left the Jews as a people actually disconnected from God, although they claimed to be within his favor. Christian triumphalism took this position because it is believed that the new covenant is the church. The church in its hierarchical forms, sacramental powers, and inspired teachings is the kingdom of God on earth. The church defines the whole scope of those who are to be saved.

The interpretation of the new covenant by Christian triumphalism represents a deformation of the covenant traditions in very crucial ways. Most important, the various covenants do not abrogate or replace one another. The prior covenants are the context of the later ones. As Paul said, "For the gifts and the call of God are irrevocable" (Rom. 11:29). The covenant of disclosure formed through Abraham did not replace the earlier covenant in Noah or Adam that had been formed with all of humankind. The covenant of disclosure illumines the way in which God works in his larger covenant of salvation. Similarly, the church did not replace Israel in the covenant of disclosure. Instead, the church, to use the biblical image, is "a wild olive shoot" grafted in to share "the richness of the olive tree" (Rom. 11:17–18).

The new covenant ratified in Jesus is a covenant of the future to which his life and ministry point. The function of the church is to form a witnessing community that points to the saving work of God throughout all creation, so that men and women may join in it. The responsibility of the Christian is in witnessing to that pattern of redemption, that form of the divine name, given in Jesus Christ by which the future is to be shaped. But its existence does not define the outer limits of the saving activity of God. The church is the herald of the kingdom but is not identical with it.

Christian triumphalism springs also from the rejection of the orientation in time which is characteristic of the covenant traditions of the Bible. Triumphalism asserts that the kingdom is already here and that the church with its message and sacraments provides the only means of entrance into it. Triumphalism is based upon a realized, not a futuristic, eschatology. The glories of the kingdom and its powers are transferred to the church. By contrast, in the New Testament, the new covenant, or covenant of the kingdom of God, has been ratified in the life, death, and resurrection of Jesus, but its full actuality is in the future. Now an intimation of its meaning or a sharing in its powers is possible. People may enjoy its "first fruits" or share in the "earnest" or "down-payment" of its full reality by the presence of the Holy Spirit (2 Cor. 1:22; 5:5; Eph. 1:12–14). But it remains a kingdom which is to come in the future. What has been granted in Jesus is the name, or pattern of new being, by which people identify and articulate the presence of the kingdom in the midst of the ambiguities of their present life.

The new covenant is symbolic of a level of existence that transcends religiousness. According to Jeremiah, "And no longer shall each man teach his neighbor, saying, 'Know the Lord,' for they shall all know me . . . " (Jer. 31:34). The Law of God is within all people, so that religious instruction and cultus are unnecessary. There is no more temple, in the Christian vision of the future (Rev. 21:22). In its most thoroughgoing form the vision of completion excludes the need for any mediator between God and humankind. The mediation between transcendent reality and the sinful and finite life of the world, which is expressed for Christianity through Jesus as the Son of God, will become a thing of the past with the full actualization of the kingdom. "When all things are subjected to him then the Son himself will also be subjected to him who put all things under him, that God may be all in all" (1 Cor. 15:28).

When the contradiction caused by sin and death is overcome, all the religious symbols, acts, and institutions that are needed to remind humankind of the reality of the transcendent have become obsolete. Even the principle of a human-divine mediation is uncalled for in the new covenant of immediacy. Religion is a temporary aspect of human existence made necessary by the contradictions that characterize this present age. But in their highest expression the covenants point to the transcending of religions, not the absolutizing of any particular religion.

IV

This analysis of the covenant traditions of Christianity provides the means for dealing with the particularity and universality of Christianity in new ways. Three motifs emerge as germane to this question: (1) The rethinking of the nature of monotheism. (2) The disclosure of the nature of God's redemptive work. (3) The translation of Jesus' name.

1. The radical monotheism implicit in the covenant traditions means that God as known in Christian faith is not simply a tribal or communal god now given universality. Rather in the revelatory events of this faith, the particularity of its vision of God has been transformed. God is not ultimately known as "my god" or "our god," although he has chosen a particular people to serve his purposes. Finally he is not simply known as "the God of Abraham, Isaac, and Jacob," but as "Yahweh," the transcendent One, whose cultic name, "Yahweh," is interpreted to mean "I cause to be what I cause to be." The particularity of his self-disclosure is always linked to the universality of his sovereignty (Exod. 3:13–15).

The transcendence of God is not in his aloofness but in his freedom to act in judgment and redemption. As "God of gods" or "Lord of lords," Yahweh calls into question the ways in which his covenant people misunderstand and misuse his name. God in his freedom is the One who breaks in from beyond to call into question even those through whom he reveals himself. The covenanted peoples are the means of his self-disclosure but not its limit. Even when elected to be the means of revelation, a people do not control God nor create his presence. He is still God the Lord over against his own people.

The freedom of God is most clearly shown in the death and resurrection of Jesus. In Jesus Christ, God is revealed not as the Protector God who saved his Elect One, his Son, from death, nor his elect people from suffering. Rather God is revealed as the God of resurrection who creates new possibilities beyond the power of death itself. Not only are geographical boundaries overcome; so is the ultimate boundary between being and nonbeing overcome by God. This transcendent One is free to create whatever possibilities for responding to him that he wishes. Human beings do not create the possibility of responding to him nor does the proclamation of any religious tradition create his presence. God reaches beyond our time and place to create new being where none could be thought to exist.

In his freedom the one God is present in the world already. The preaching of the Christian message provides the means for responding to his presence. It does not create that presence. For this reason, Christians may affirm the legitimacy of responses to God through religious traditions other than their own. This is not simply the usual grudging affirmation given by Christians who refer to the non-Christian traditions as "the extraordinary means of grace." Rather, as Hans Küng has rightfully pointed out, the non-Christian religions are "the ordinary means of grace" for the vast majority of humankind. [6]

To affirm the possibility of responding to God's creative and redemptive presence through a variety of religious traditions raises a question. Does this affirmation mean that all religious traditions are, in some sense, equally true or good? The answer is clearly "no." Religion is a form of human activity that is open to all of the ambiguities of human existence. Religion has taken destructive as well as creative forms. To affirm that a variety of traditions provide a means for actualizing God's presence implies the need for a basis for the discernment of authentic responses. This basis for discernment comes from an explication of the nature of God's redemptive work from within the revelatory circle of Christian faith. In other words, what perspective does Christian faith give on the ambiguities of human religiousness?

2. The new covenant ratified in Jesus Christ reveals fully not only the freedom of God but also the form of God's presence. God is in the world to be "for" humankind. His work is a work of fulfilling human life. Not only in his blessings but also in his judgments, God is "for us" because he is driving human beings from the radical self-centeredness that deforms and denies our human existence. The judgment of God is not irrational anger. As the prophets make clear his blessings are not the reward for performing magical rituals but in conforming all human life to his justice. As the God of justice, God is "for us" because he provides the way by which human kind may be fulfilled, by living according to his will. But for Chris-

tians, the fullest disclosure of the relationship of God to the fulfillment of human existence is given in Jesus. He is confessed to be God incarnate. He is the Second Person of the Trinity, existing in a fully human form. The divine Logos has become literally "enfleshed" according to the Fourth Gospel (John 1:14). For this reason, Karl Barth can speak, as a Christian theologian, of "the humanity of God." "God requires no exclusion of humanity, no nonhumanity, not to speak of inhumanity, in order to be truly God. . . . His deity *encloses humanity in itself.*" This high vision of human nature does not spring from an optimistic judgment of humankind now. "It is due him because he is the being whom God willed to exalt as His covenant-partner, not otherwise."[7]

In Jesus Christ, God shows how the relationship to him fulfills human life. What this means is that wherever there is found that new being that fulfills human nature, it is a witness to the saving work of God. Christians acknowledge and receive this work of humanization as the work of God, although the name of Jesus may not be specifically known or confessed in every place that new being is found. They are able to do this because they believe that "God was in Christ reconciling the world unto himself" (2 Cor. 5:19). In knowing Jesus, Christian faith is provided with the *canon*—the measuring stick—by which the activity of God may be discerned and confessed because it is Christ through whom this salvation is ultimately given.

Christians have differed widely in identifying the sources of human goodness and fulfillment for those who stand outside of their particular faith. One tradition in Christian theology has held that the only real virtue is that which comes from a conscious relationship to Christ and the church, while others have argued for the existence of natural sources of virtue that exist apart from Christian faith. Christian triumphalism has followed a tradition formulated by Augustine, who argued that the virtues of the pagans are but "splendid vices."[8] The best that Augustine could say was that in pursuit of certain vices (the attaining of human glory) other vices (civil disorder and debauchery) were restrained. But to follow the logic of this position would lead to a rejection of the radical monotheism of biblical religion, or it would be to make the fatal mistake of calling goodness evil. Where human life is being renewed and virtue expressed, there the work of God is being actualized. Where human life is debased or destroyed, the work of God is being rejected, even when religious traditions, including those of Christianity, are being invoked. The christological norm is a principle of judgment against Christianity as well as other religions.

God's presence may be actualized through many religious traditions. The form this actualization takes is the renewal and fulfillment of human existence. Christians believe that there is ultimately only one source of goodness, although there are different ways in which this power for goodness may be actualized. The criterion for this actualization for Christian faith is the new being revealed in Jesus Christ. The fulfilled human existence revealed in Jesus Christ unfolded in response to the unique presence of God in him. So wherever human life is being fulfilled it is a sign of the presence of God. But in actualizing that new being God expresses his freedom to be "for us" by creating opportunities for new being throughout his creation.

3. Having moved this far, the sticking point remains: What is to be made of the Christian claim that other than Jesus Christ "there is no other name under heaven given among men by which we must be saved" (Acts 4:12). For Christian faith "Jesus" is the name by which the nature and activity of God is fully revealed. His name is the saving name because it affords the means by which human beings share in the grace and love that is the nature of God himself. The central intellectual, institutional, and spiritual problem of Christianity is that of exactly how to share this name with others. How can the "name of Jesus" be given expression in proclamation, liturgy, ethics, or community life? The intellectual history of Christianity has been determined by the struggle to give the "name of Jesus" expression in differing cultures and worldviews. Two possibilities for dealing with this problem were excluded by the early church. First, the "name of Jesus" is not a kind of

magical formula whose very utterance looses the powers of salvation. The ethical, antimagical dimensions of Christian faith brought about the rejection of that option very early in Christian history (Acts 19:11–20). The "name of Jesus" is not a piece of secret *gnosis* as in the docetic savior myths of Gnosticism. Second, the "name of Jesus" cannot be adequately expressed through a particular legal code or ideological program whose acceptance would assure salvation. In its rejection of legalism the early church foreclosed that possibility, although many later Christians tried to create new legalism in the name of Jesus (Gal. 2:11–3:1). Salvation comes from a self-abandoning trust which is called "faith."

The "name of Jesus" is the disclosure of the pattern of God's action in human salvation. As such, it is open to translation. This "name" may be translated or given fresh expression in differing times and places. It is not in the continuity of a verbalism but in faithfulness to its meaning that the saving power revealed in Jesus is actualized. This is true because the "name of Jesus" is the disclosure of the structure of new being. It is the pattern of salvation. So the universality of Christianity is grounded in the translatability of the "name of Jesus," not in the imposition of particular formularies on others. This power of new being operates throughout the world under the names of many religious traditions. It is recognized and celebrated by Christians because they know its pattern or meaning through Jesus of Nazareth.

For Christian faith the "name of Jesus" is defined by his life, death, and resurrection. The "name" is the encoding of a pattern of existence by which new being is actualized. It is a pattern of existence marked by a movement from abnegation to fulfillment, from death to resurrection. Jesus revealed the shape of new being already in his words about the need for dying to the self to find the true self. "Whoever cares for his own safety is lost; but if a man will let himself be lost for my sake, he will find his true self" (Matt. 16:25, NEB). Supremely he revealed this pattern of finding life through dying to the self in his own death on the cross.

An early Christian hymn brings this fundamental metaphor

of salvation to expression as it celebrates the salvation given in Jesus. "For the divine nature was his from the first; yet he did not think to snatch equality with God, but made himself nothing, assuming the nature of a slave." The saving action of the Christ was in giving up his place of glory; unlike Satan he did not seek equality with God. The saving action is self-negation, not self-assertion. But even foreswearing his heavenly prerogatives was not the end. Now in his human existence, the Christ becomes obedient to death. "Bearing the human likeness, revealed in human shape, he humbled himself, and in obedience accepted even death—death on a cross" (Phil. 2:5–8, NEB). Then in his resurrection-exaltation, he receives the seal of the divine approval, the fulfillment of his true self. He received the divine name and is to be worshipped to the glory of God the Father (2:9–11). The worship due him is the willingness to accept dying to the self as the way to life. The faithful person is told, "Have this mind in you which you have in Christ Jesus" (2:5). It is the mind of one who seeks to live by self-forgetting abnegation, not by demonic self-assertion. This way of finding life is universal. It embraces all levels of reality (2:10).

The pattern of new being encoded in the "name of Jesus" is one that is encountered in many religious traditions. Christians identify it and celebrate it because of what they know through Jesus Christ. Other traditions live out of this power of new being in accordance with the names by which they encounter and participate in ultimate reality. This does not make them crypto Christians or members of "a hidden" or "latent church." They are and remain what they are —Hindus, Buddhists, Muslims, or devotees of a myriad of other religions. This is possible because the "name of Jesus" is translatable. The "name of Jesus" is the encoding of the motif of death and resurrection as the key to new being. This motif is brought to expression in vastly different ways in various religions as they become vehicles for human renewal and fulfillment. But the crucial thing in identifying the "name of Jesus" is not in the verbalisms, but in the underlying pattern of new being at work.

There is an irony locked up in the Christian claim to the finality of Jesus Christ. It is that Christians want to apply the finality of Jesus Christ as a judgment on every other religion but not on themselves. The finality of Jesus Christ is in the unconditioned way in which he points beyond himself, even to the point of surrendering his personal selfhood, so that humankind may find healing in the Unconditioned. Just this is his Godlikeness, his divinity, if you will. The Christian religion will receive new life when it is willing to die to the demonic forms its claim to finality has taken. It will then enter fully into the power of the "name of Jesus." Christians must be willing to accept the death of their ideologies to enter into the resurrection of new being.

NOTES

1. Modern critical historical scholarship has helped to illumine the process by which the covenant idea became a factor in the faith of ancient Israel and the church. While there can be no final exactitude on this question, it would seem that the covenant idea entered the religion of Israel at the time of Moses, although it had its roots in the patriarchal age. For the history of covenant theology in ancient Israel see George E. Mendenhall, *Law and Covenant in Israel and the Ancient Near East* (Pittsburgh: The Biblical Colloquium, 1955), pp. 24–41, and also his article "Covenant," *Interpreter's Dictionary of the Bible*, ed. George Buttrick (New York: Abingdon Press, 1962), 1:714–23. The line of argumentation in this paper is not dependent upon the historical reconstruction of how the covenant idea emerged. Rather the argument proceeds from the final recension of these texts in the form given them in canonical Scripture as accepted as authoritative in the Jewish and Christian communities. The crucial questions for this paper arise out of the meaning of Scripture in its canonical shape as it functions as authoritative in the church. Hence the argument for the primacy of the covenant in Noah derives from the order given the covenants in the canonical shape of the Scriptures, rather than in any putative historical reconstruction of how the covenant theology emerged.

2. The basic account of how the covenant theology was distorted by Christian triumphalism is found in Adolf Harnack, *The Mission and Expansion of Christianity* (New York: Harper & Brothers, 1961), pp. 65–72 and 279–89.

3. Gerhard von Rad, *Genesis: A Commentary* (Philadelphia: Westminster Press, 1961), pp. 129–30.

4. Jean Daniélou, *Holy Pagans of the Old Testament* (London: Longman, Green, 1957), pp. 76–85, 90, and 127–35. This term has also been given explication by Raimundo Panikkar, "Eine Betrachtung über Melkisedek, *Kairos* 1 (1959), pp. 5–17.

5. H. Richard Neibuhr, *Radical Monotheism and Western Culture* (New York: Harper & Brothers, 1960), pp. 1–37.

6. Hans Küng, "The World Religions in God's Plan of Salvation," in *Christian Revelation and World Religions*, ed. Joseph Neuner (London: Burns & Oates, 1967), pp. 51–53.

7. Karl Barth, *The Humanity of God* (Richmond: John Knox Press, 1960), pp. 50–52.

8. Augustine, *The City of God*, V: 12ff. and XIX: 25.

2

A Buddhist Response:

Religion Beyond Ideology and Power

Mahinda Palihawadana

My task is, in the words of the sponsors of this symposium, to make "a response from a Buddhist point of view" to Professor Dawe's analysis and vision. I have been trying to clarify to myself what would be a Buddhist point of view in the context of this assignment. My first conclusion was that any reasoned response that I make, being one born and bred in an environment that is happy to regard itself as Buddhist, and being one who is happy to be the product of such an environment, would meet the criterion of a Buddhist response. That conclusion should stand. But, at the same time, it seems to me to be important to add that I am not proceeding from a consciousness of any particular Buddhist point of view that I feel bound to uphold. In the end, I can speak from no other than my personal point of view. But I shall try to be especially mindful of what would be the Buddhist conception of living rightly in our beleaguered planet in this age and time.

I

May I begin my response with a few general observations? Both in East and West, religious societies present a rather perplexing picture today. We are all aware of the familiar signs of "sickness" in these societies: erosion of observance, slackening of faith, loss of prestige of the elites, and so on.

Yet, this is only one side of the picture. On the other side, we have evidence of their basic strengths that have elicited profound attachments. Each one of them has come to be viewed as a treasured possession by its adherents and has in turn conferred on them a sense of identity and a civilizing worldview. Their toughness of fiber is demonstrable by their resistance to conversion. Equally impressive has been their resilience and adaptability. At issue, then, is not whether religious societies are becoming extinct, but rather this problem: Which is the more significant, their signs of sickness or their continuing dynamism?

These two together, however, hardly leave in doubt the fact that religious societies have the will to live and the hope of continued life, even though there is turmoil in their souls. In the reservoir of power that the religious societies represent, the *positive factor* is this will to live. But the turmoil in the soul indicates the presence of a *negative factor* as well: elements of weakness that new challenges have brought into consciousness.

What are the challenges?

Overtly by political action and covertly through modern education, attempts are being made to impose new worldviews on religious societies. These and other developments are producing, in religious circles, an awareness of enemies hard to subjugate and a crisis of confidence. In this situation, will a society's reactions not be similar to those of individuals suddenly confronted with an awareness of their weaknesses? The least they owe to themselves is to demonstrate their strengths. To go down, as if they were no good at all, would produce the greatest guilt, the worst sense of self-betrayal.

In much the same way, the impact of science, political creeds, and the other religions is compelling the religions of the world to search their souls.[1] If, at first, these appeared to be rivals and foes, increasingly now the confrontation is changing in character. If the challengers' first move evoked a posture of defense, their second move seems to evoke internal adjustments. Will what is to follow not change the challengers as much as it may change the challenged?

Though each of the religions has provided a worldview by which men and women lived, can any one of them claim to be perfect? They have all failed in one way or another. Most notably, they have failed to make people live up to their ideals. So the challenge of the other religions may make us ask ourselves: "Are our ideals unattainable or unrealistic? Have we somewhere in our history failed to take note of important aspects of the tradition? How to account for our obvious failures?"

Buddhists, noting that Christian societies generally have been the pioneers in advancing to massive economic successes, in eradicating disease, in achieving technological triumphs, might conceivably feel that they should seriously examine the Christian critique of what has been regarded as Buddhist pessimism, or even the basic position accorded to *dukkha* (woe or suffering) in the Buddhist view of humanity. It may be argued that it is "constitutionally" difficult for Buddhists to develop an attitude of conquering nature and of facing up to the intractable challenges of hunger, disease, deprivation, etc. Will the Buddhists accept this criticism meekly, without a serious re-examination of the meaning of the doctrine of *dukkha*? Obviously not. No one can forecast what such re-examination will bring. But whatever it brings, it is likely to lead to religious revitalization, either via healthy changes or via healthy rediscoveries or both.

Academic students of religion have hardly to be told that in their long histories the religions have undergone more changes, or more drastic changes, than the faithful are likely to concede. It remains a task for future religious consciousness to admit this fact squarely and to be ready to take the consequences. Some fear that granting respectability to a principle of change in religious viewpoints and attitudes will be self-destructive. But, in fact, the recognition of "changing religion" may contribute to a religion's survival, as probably it was in this way they actually survived.

I think then that by religious change, the great traditions

strengthen one another by various forms of "cross-fertilization." Attitudes and teachings cannot be bodily taken from one tradition and planted in another, but the strengths of one tradition may become the "conducive factor"[2] for another tradition to examine itself. Through this interaction traditions may generate new strengths in terms of their own resources.

Thus it seems to me probable that in the next stage of the encounter of religions each tradition will internally wrestle with the weak or "negative" side of its development. At that stage, it should appear to each tradition that it owes a serious duty to itself to inquire: "What have we to propose to humankind? Has humankind seriously taken account of what our tradition has been proposing? Have *we* been taking what was proposed in the past seriously enough? Or have we drifted on to a less serious course of action, or even moved in the opposite direction?" As each tradition reviews itself, there will be at least three important "negative developments" for each tradition to cope with internally: (1) dogmatism, (2) institutionalism, and (3) alliance with power and wealth. Religious traditions must learn to divest themselves of these "cankers" in order to advance to a new creative phase.

II

The sense of urgency that informs Professor Dawe's paper —and indeed, behind this entire symposium—is acknowledgedly one that derives from the problems of our time.

Throughout centuries of its existence, Christian faith flourished in a religiously plural world. Christianity has not only lived but sought aggressively to expand for at least five centuries now. And yet interfaith colloquy is a phenomenon of but yesterday. What is more, it is still largely Christian-inspired. Why this should be so is surely an interesting moot point. The very fact that Christians sit down with others to contemplate their mutual existence is an index of the unusual situation.

It is my feeling that, for reasons stemming largely from their historical situation (the greater violence exerted on others; the greater resources and opportunities for intellectual concerns; the greater disenchantment with material power that others are still only aspiring to achieve, etc.), the Christians more than the others are consciously moving toward what I called above the second stage in the encounter of the religions of the world.

Professor Dawe's exercise in the rethinking of the relationship of Christianity to the other religions fits into this context. Here he specifically examines several cherished old dogmas in the course of an excursion into the "possibilities within Christianity."

To me it is a very encouraging sign that Professor Dawe's examination of the role of the doctrine of covenant and his related discussion leads him to the conclusion that "Christians must be willing to accept the death of their ideologies to enter into the resurrection of new being."

Ideology, or the body of dogmas that induces and justifies a particular power relationship, has exerted an especially pernicious effect in the religious history of humankind. The process begins by a simple translation of religious teachings into a "property" that satisfies the most primitive weakness of the human soul: self-centeredness. Almost every religious teaching known has suffered this fate. From a call to action, it gets changed into a dogma of which one can say: "This is mine and by it I shall be distinguished" and also: "This is the thing to believe." This in itself contains the seed of divisiveness. How much more so if we go on to think: "This is the superior vision and it must prevail," no matter what the cost.

We can encounter the first development in all the faiths of humankind. But evidently it had an unusual degree of significance in Christianity. "In the Christian case, the role of belief has been quite major, at times decisive. Doctrine has been a central expression of faith, often a criterion of it. . . . For the Christian Church, theology has been a conspicuously important matter."[3]

I tend to think that "doctrine" carries with it an inherent capacity to lend itself to misdirection.[4] The misdirection becomes obvious when doctrine develops the extension that it must be imposed, even by force of arms. It has been pointed out that this ideological aggressiveness is one of the special features of Christianity.[5]

In view of this, the conclusion to which Dawe's thinking has led him is revolutionary, though perhaps not impossible to expect in the present climate of the creative agony of the Christian consciousness.

While I value this central thrust of Professor Dawe's thesis, I am also a little disconcerted in one respect. This has something to do with his words "the relationship of Christianity to other religions" in a key sentence of the paper. I do not want to be a stickler for unvarying accuracy of words, and I have no quarrel with the word "Christianity" as such. But it is important to know what precisely "Christianity" stands for in this particular context. As it is, the word seems to convey this meaning: the institutionalized "religion" built up by the activities of the Christian church in its various forms over the centuries. "Christian faith" appearing in the title of this symposium suggests quite different connotations. I am not sure whether Professor Dawe intentionally makes a distinction and thinks that Christianity is the more appropriate word as far as his thesis is concerned.

Why I feel ill at ease with "Christianity" has something to do with religious institutionalism in the broad sense. In my mind, institutionalism invariably raises associations of dogmatism and ideological authoritarianism.

Humanity needs institutions, but, at the same time, we should not have to surrender our right to creative individual thought. Where institutions encroach on this necessary freedom, we have institutionalism, and this is a "negative factor" that all religious movements have the tendency to develop. The negative element is not in institutions as such, but in a particular relationship that is usually allowed to grow between individual and institution.

There is a specific individual task that no church can take over. It is only by performing that task that one can do the little that is within one's power to help the world.[6]

In the history of the Buddhist movement, too, what I admire most is the stage when it was comparatively "un-organized."[7] I must confess that I am no admirer of the tremendous power

and efficiency ascribed to the organized church in Christendom. Since ideology and institutionalism are necessary allies,
it seems to be a corollary of Professor Dawe's thesis that
institutionalism also deserves to be devalued today.

Perhaps the development of liberal thought in the West has
advanced so far that no special effort is needed to reduce the
dangers of institutional authority at the present time. My
Buddhist background certainly makes me feel uneasy about
Christians for whom this is not the case. It seems to me that far
less damage would have been done to the Christian image had
the movement been less institutionalized and more divorced
from power. Less institutionalization would, for example,
have led to less "denativization" of Christianized Asians and
Africans. This loss of cultural identity is one of the least pleas-
ant effects of the spread of the Christian movement in the
world. [8]

In view of this, I would like to ask: "Does it also not lie
among the possibilities within Christianity to replace its pre-
dilection for institutional power with a preference for real
spiritual power, which one must suppose was the source of its
original strength?"

It is however, a given fact of the present historical situation
that Christianity and Christian societies in general have at
their disposal a vast reservoir of temporal power. This brings
me to the next point that I wish to make in response to Professor Dawe.

The strain between the Christian communities of the world
and the non-Christian communities is not only due to the
theological distance between them but also in considerable
measure due to their power relationship. While the Christian
part of humankind is, by and large, affluent, the non-
Christian, with a few exceptions, is poverty-stricken. While
the one wields power, the other lacks and, of course, aspires to
power. In this context, power is connotative of accumulated
wealth, on one hand, and potential violence, on the other.

Professor Dawe's critical appraisal of the theology of covenant can be helpful in dealing with any theological arguments
supporting a power relationship that favors a particular people

or group as the "holy people of God." There are great potentialities in Christian thought for correcting misconceptions on
the power imbalance. Exploring these potentialities is impera-
tive in a world where 80 percent of humanity lives in dire
poverty, and the affluent have almost all the instruments to
perpetuate that disproportionate distribution or, worse, to
make the distribution even more disproportionate.

That exercise should also come "from within . . . Christian
faith and tradition" rather than from without. However, one
might be excused for adding a few footnotes in anticipation.

It is in that spirit that I quote a biblical passage that you will
remember only too well, and I quote it without any "Third
World" self-righteousness. This is a passage that genuinely
speaks to my heart. It is one worth repeating a thousand times:

And when he was gone forth into the way, there came one running,
and kneeled to him and asked him, Good Master, what shall I do that
I may inherit eternal life?

And Jesus said unto him, Why callest thou me good? There is none
good but one, that is, God.

Thou knowest the commandments, Do not commit adultery, Do
not kill, Do not steal, Do not bear false witness, Defraud not, Honor
thy father and mother.

And he answered and said unto him, Master, all those I have
observed from my youth.

Then Jesus beholding him, loved him and said unto him, One thing
thou lackest: go thy way, sell whatsoever thou hast, and give to the
poor, and thou shalt have treasure in heaven: and come, and take up
the cross and follow me.

And he was sad at that saying and went away grieved: for he had
great possessions.

And Jesus looked around about, and saith unto his disciples, How
hardly shall they that have riches enter into the kingdom of God!

And the disciples were astonished at his words. But Jesus an-
swereth again, and saith unto them, Children, how hard is it for them
that trust in riches to enter into the kingdom of God!

It is easier for a camel to go through the eye of a needle than for a
rich man to enter into the kingdom of God.

And they were astonished out of measure, saying among themselves, who then can be saved? [Mark 10:17–26.]

The comment of H. G. Wells on this passage is well taken.

In view of what he plainly said is it any wonder that all who were rich and prosperous felt a horror of strange things, a swimming of their world at his teaching? He was dragging out all the little private reservations they had made from social service into the light of a universal religious life. He was like some terrible moral huntsman digging mankind out of the snug burrows in which they had lived hitherto. In the white blaze of this kingdom of his there was to be no property, no privilege, no pride and precedence; no motive indeed and no reward but love. Is it any wonder that men were dazzled and blinded and cried out against him?[9]

We are all aware that voices are heard today from different parts of Christendom that have awakened to this "revolutionary" spirit of early Christianity. It is a spirit as relevant now as it was nearly two thousand years ago. These voices calling for change might have been easier to stifle in the not so distant past. Today it is not possible to stifle them, even on the basis of self-interest. We live in a world where it seems less than likely that the richest will continue to be regarded as the most favored children of the Lord. Would not some poor primitives of an unheard-of wilderness inherit the earth after a nuclear holocaust of the future, if ever one comes?

III

It could be argued that there is need today for at least some compelling new worldview, as an expedient to direct aright the energies of a world threatened by violence and divisiveness that it has irreligiously allowed to gather within itself.

If we can use the word "theology" for such a worldview, we may say that what we need is a theology "for survival and equal develement." We all have a responsibility for removing the obstacles to the development of such a theology, although perhaps those of us with the greater power have also the greater responsibility. It is the powerful who are also the more vulnerable to criticism. Professor Dawe's essay is surely one that bespeaks the conscious acceptance of that responsibility.

Our critical self-examination can never come to an end. Is it going to be easy to translate a "survival theology" into a practical way of life? Will it be easy for those among us who are more powerful to resist the temptation of wanting our nation to become or to remain the most powerful in the world? Will we be able to stay without over-exploiting the resources available to humankind? Will we be willing to live without exploiting the weaknesses of the weak or without manipulating the market to the disadvantage of the producer of raw-materials? Will we be able to resist over-filling the arsenals of the nations with the most lethal and sophisticated weapons of destruction?

It needs no prophetic skill to say that it will not be easy. But religious people are, even in spite of what they professly believe, optimists as a rule. [10] Hence we can agree that we will turn back, but perhaps only after approaching the edge of the precipice from where we will have a more horrendous view of the abyss. Perhaps our turning will only come as we glimpse the abyss we are intellectually sure is awaiting our eyes. Let us hope that in that eleventh hour at least our religious education will hasten our conversion.

NOTES

1. I share Professor W.C. Smith's concern over the use of the word "religion." To use it in the traditional way is to perpetuate a fiction. "Faith" or "religious tradition" would be preferable, in that they do not connote *rigidity* or *defined frontiers* and in that they (at least partially) succeed in evoking the senses of flux and elasticity that properly must be associated with the content of religiousness. Unfortunately, these words do not fit in so well in certain contexts (as in the above). And yet we need some word to indicate the relatedness of individuals religiously within the realms of what have been called Buddhism, Christianity, and so on. Hence I continue using "religion," but meaning by it an "entity" that actually keeps on changing in form and content.

2. Enlightening in this respect is one of the "conditions" listed in the Buddhist teaching of causation, *atthi-paccaya,* or "presence-condition": " . . . a phenomenon . . . which through its presence is a condition to other phenomena" (Nyanatiloka, *Buddhist Dictionary* [Colombo: Frewin,1950], p. 105).

3. W.C. Smith, "Faith and Belief," University of Toronto Public Lecture, January 9, 1968, unpublished paper, p. 15.

4. This may be due to my Buddhist background. The Buddha considered rigid doctrinal positions to be "a wilderness, a puppet-show, a writing and a fetter," which are "coupled with misery, ruin, despair, and agony." Thus, "this that is called doctrine is something that the Tathagata has quit" *(Majjhima Nikāya,* Sutta 72).

It must be sadly admitted, however, that the lesson of this thinking was not fully assimilated by the Buddhists, who went on to build a strong attachment to what were called "right views." Right views cannot be objected to, so long as they are not allowed to develop into a "property" to be defended against others. But human weakness prevailed, and this development did take place, though perhaps not to the same extent as in Christianity.

5. Dawe himself refers to it. See also A.J. Toynbee, *An Historian's Approach to Religion* (London: Oxford University Press, 1956), annex 18, pp. 251–52. Toynbee goes as far as to say that the fanatical vein in communism and fascism is a direct continuation of a Palestinian legacy.

6. This should be the implication of the Buddhist idea of personal salvation. There can strictly be no such thing as a private enlightenment. The Buddha's own enlightenment is one of the least private events in world history. Toynbee seems to express this in a typically Christian idiom when he says: "It is through His love and pity, much more than through His insight into the means of release from the suffering by which His pity and love were evoked, that the Buddha is still alive and at work in the World today" *(Historian's Approach,* p. 72).

7. "The whole trend of early Buddhism was . . . anti-authoritarian. The keynote is struck in the Mahāparinibbāna Suttanta, where the Buddha calls upon the Bhikkhus to be . . . as lamps . . . unto yourselves, with yourselves . . . as your refuge" (Sukumar Dutt, *Early Buddhist Monachism*

[Bombay: Asia Publishing House, 1960], p. 159). Cf. also Walpola Rahula, *History of Buddhism in Ceylon* (Colombo: M.D. Gunasena, 1956), p. 171: "First there is no leader or head of the Sangha. But the members . . . would always respect and follow any monk who is virtuous, wise and learned. Secondly there is no centralization of authority and power. They maintained their unity and discipline as groups in different areas."

8. The organized church was wedded to the temporal power of the colonial governments. The denativization of the inhabitants of the conquered lands greatly helped the colonial adventure. The spiritual effort of convinced individuals, divorced from temporal power, could scarcely have led to denativization. Divorced from temporal power after decolonization, Christians are profoundly concerned, especially at an individual level, to renativize themselves culturally, without discarding the Christian heritage that they have acquired. (The activities of the Study Centre for Religion and Society in Colombo and the Tulana Centre for Research and Encounter, Kelaniya, are examples of the intellectual aspect of such a movement in Sri Lanka, with no evident "institutional" support.)

9. H.G. Wells, *A Short History of the World* (Harmondsworth, Eng.: Penguin Books, 1960), p. 157.

10. From a strictly Buddhist point of view, there is no guarantee that we will change our ways; we may, if we have not engrossed ourselves with greed and hate beyond the probable point of return. It cannot be said that humanity is structurally incapable of going past the edge of the precipice and into the abyss below.

3

A Hindu Response:

The Value of Religious Pluralism

K. L. Seshagiri Rao

I wish to record my appreciation and gratitude for Professor Dawe's thoughtful and constructive presentation on the theme: "Christian Faith in a Religiously Plural World." His paper goes directly to the heart of the problem and faces the inconvenient issues boldly. It discusses the "paradox of religion," which releases love and aggression, sacrifice and hatred at the same time in differing human contexts. Specifically, Professor Dawe makes an agonizing reappraisal of certain Christian attitudes that foment religious hatred and violence. He deplores the fact that the fury of religious animosity is often let loose not only against other communities of faith but also against the followers of different sects within the Christian faith. He rightly asserts: "This is a price humankind is no longer willing or able to pay." He then raises a practical question: "How is release to be found from the destructiveness associated with this religion, while still keeping open its power to enlarge and enhance human life?" Next, he wrestles theologically to find "new ways for the Christian community to relate the particularity and universality of its faith."

A prominent feature of our times is the unprecedented mingling of peoples of different races, cultures, and religious traditions on a global scale. This phenomenon has brought to the attention of thinking people all over the world the inescapable fact of interdependence of nations and the solidarity of humankind. Although religious seers and prophets have all along upheld the essential unity of the human race, it has nevertheless taken a long time for humankind to arrive at even a notional acknowledgement of that unity. In the secular world, this has come about partly as a result of the holocausts of two world wars and is being reinforced now by the instant communication of worldwide news. Faint glimpses of the emerging world community are seen sometimes at the U.N., UNESCO, the World Food Organization, and other international organizations.

On the religious front, confrontation has given place to contact; there is a move from mutual recrimination to religious conversation. The multi-religious situation of our times has made inter-religious dialogue a serious concern. The pressures of pluralistic societies compel us to look at our respective religious traditions in the light of others. They demand a reconsideration of our attitudes to peoples of other faiths. Indeed, we are now passing through a process of self-understanding, self-searching, and self-criticism. We are witnesses to and participants in this rethinking process.

Physicians are supposed to cure and not spread disease. Religious traditions are not supposed to spread hatred, intolerance, and violent conflict against one another. They are meant to be forces of reconciliation. In practice though, they have often functioned and still function as divisive forces. They have stressed sectarian trends, and they have raised walls of separation between people. But such parochial attitudes cannot satisfy humankind as a whole in the present-day world. The time has come for the different religious traditions to make a new departure. Confronted as they are with profound problems of human survival and destiny, they have both the responsibility and the opportunity to repent for their past, forgive one another for their acts of commission and omission, and cooperate with each other in the promotion of human community and well-being. There are differences between them, and will continue to be; they should be respected and preserved. But there are also universal teachings and extensive resources in each tradition that can bind divisions and build bridges of understanding. They can and should foster human fellowship and world community. For what serious significance can a particular tradition have, when human existence itself loses all meaning? Unless harmonious relationships based on mutual reverence are developed among the great religions of the world, none of them can hope to be a fit instrument for creating and sustaining world community.

As inhabitants of this planet, the adherents of different faiths are bound by a common destiny. Loyalty to our respective religious traditions and communities should not undermine world community. Each religious tradition has to take a global view of things; it should realize the implications of interdependence in moral and spiritual realms also. Religious commitment should not become confinement in a system of thought or culture. To preserve and enrich the quality of life for all human beings is the common responsibility of all religious traditions. Indeed, multi-religious dialogue and cooperation have become an urgent necessity in many parts of the world. It is the theological recognition and validation of the phenomenon that have to be worked out.

Traditional theology, developed in religious isolation, has now become obsolete. The attitude of "Christian triumphalism," as Professor Dawe calls it, does not permit the different religious traditions to live side by side in friendly cooperation. Rivalry and competition between the followers of different faiths have become tragic and pointless; they have led to massacres, wars, and genocide. There is no basis to expect the displacement of all others by a single religious tradition. As far as we can see, human community will continue to be religiously pluralistic. Theology should come to terms with this fact, and attempt to do justice to the religious experience of humankind as a whole. It should open up, by a deep and thorough investigation of its heritage, a new spiritual horizon hospitable to the faiths of other people. The tradition of opposition to other faiths should yield to one of cooperation. The future usefulness of any religious tradition depends on its ability to cooperate with other traditions of humankind.

During November–December 1975, I attended the Fifth Assembly of the World Council of Churches at Nairobi, Africa, as a guest. The Assembly was remarkable in several respects and carried important implications for Christianity as a world religion. Let me mention here one of its significant features: It was the first World Council Assembly to invite guests from other religious traditions—one each from Judaism, Hinduism, Buddhism, Islam, and Sikhism. I was the guest from the Hindu faith. As I participated in the Assembly, I was reminded of Dr. Radhakrishnan's words with reference to an earlier Assembly of the W.C.C. at Evanston: "It is our hope that this movement will be extended to the living faiths of mankind. A world civilization can grow on the basis of cooperation of religions. It will broaden our vision of divine activity in life and free us from narrowness and dogmatism. All religions are our inheritance and we should not squander it away."[1] The ecumenical movement attempts to overcome conflicts within a religious tradition. Similarly, conflicts among religious traditions need to be reconciled by a "wider ecumenism" in the interests of human community and welfare.

There are difficulties involved in the ecumenical movement. There are greater difficulties in the way of achieving a "wider ecumenism." In India, as in many Asian and African countries, Christianity came into effective contact with non-Christian traditions during the days of colonial expansion of western Christendom. For all its hopes and opportunities, even today Christianity continues to be, by and large, a minority religion in these "mission lands." It has to live with and amid a majority community of another faith. Western Christians do not often fully realize the enormous cultural and national pressures faced by Christian minorities in Asia and Africa. For the Asian and African peoples, Christianity comes mixed with and vitiated by imperialism, colonial domination, racism, and even by western culture. For instance, African leaders pointed out at Nairobi that racial discrimination and economic exploitation of their continent by Christian nations are continuing realities demanding urgent remedies. In many cases, Christian groups are trying hard to eliminate the burdens of the past, to redefine their attitudes to other cultures, religions, and peoples, and to dissociate themselves from certain unhappy historical associations. They look upon Jesus Christ as Liberator from all types of oppression and injustice. However, African and Asian peoples are still handicapped in their appreciation of Christianity by what has been done to them in the past, and is being done now, by western nations.

The problems that threaten world community are not merely political and economic; they also arise from certain basic religious and spiritual attitudes. Professor Dawe deplores the attitude of "Christian triumphalism," which has been responsible for many a sad chapter in history. It is the *way* that the Gospel is presented that sometimes creates serious problems to the world community, not the Gospel itself. It is the *manner* in which Jesus Christ is communicated that creates religious dissensions, not Jesus Christ himself. It is the exclusive and imperial attitude of some Christians that threatens world community; even today it persists in some quarters. For example, a keynote speaker at the Nairobi Assembly made an eloquent plea for evangelism, and made a double reference to the 2.7 billion unevangelized peoples of the world. But he said nothing about the faiths of the people who were the "objects" of evangelism. Nor did he stop to think what difference it would make if the rest of the world also became Christian as the western world. In any case, if the faith and integrity of other persons are not respected, world community will be, at best, a dream.

The attitude frequently adopted by Christian missionaries in the eighteenth and the nineteenth centuries in relation to Hinduism was to dismiss it as a religion of crass idolatry and superstition. They did not think it worth taking seriously. They had an implicit notion that western nations possessed a superior religion and culture. Therefore, they went out to give and not to receive, to talk and not to listen. They were eager to prove the superiority or uniqueness of Christianity. The technique often adopted was to exaggerate the so-called vulnerable points in Hindu thought and practice with little appreciation of the good elements in them.

It is unfortunate that Hinduism has been a closed book all along to a majority of Christians. Such ignorance has been a breeding ground for many a wrong notion. Even the intelligentsia among Christians, by and large, lack due appreciation of the beauties of Hinduism and the sterling character of its saints and sages. Ignorance and misconception have often led to indifference or even positive contempt. Some Christian theologians see in Hinduism an invitation of the devil to draw people away from truth; they see all other religions as fundamentally "unbelief" to be displaced by Christianity. Some others admit a "point of contact" and see other revelations condescendingly as "preparatory" to Christianity. Sometimes a distinction is made between general revelation and special revelation. Hinduism, along with other non-Christian religions, is supposed to be the result of general revelation, while Christianity is said to be the result of special revelation and "the crown of Hinduism." Further, it is generally held that outside the Christian church there is no salvation.

Professor Dawe thinks that such an attitude to other religions is the result of "Christian triumphalism"; it is distorted, though obviously a part of Christian tradition. It does not reflect the "spirit" of Christianity. In my opinion, a radical change is called for in the Christian understanding of Hinduism. A "Christian" approach, in relation to other religions, should reach out, not to the worst, but to the best elements in them and should accept "the honest worship of all peoples" as the worship of God. God has left himself nowhere "without witness," and the truths revealed to the Hindus should be appreciated by Christians. Christ could be interpreted more deeply by knowing the way God has illuminated the sages of India. It is a "Christian" duty to recognize the noble elements in Hinduism.

Professor Dawe thinks that any constructive reformulation of the relationship of Christianity to other religions should fulfill certain conditions or follow certain guidelines:

1. It must "proceed from within and not without Christian faith and tradition."
2. It cannot be done on a basis that "distorts the other traditions to which it is being related."
3. It cannot be done on a basis "unintelligible to Christians."

4. It has to be related to the fact that "no particular religion is the sole religion of humankind."

The fourth condition is historically and categorically valid. Between the first and the second conditions, I see a degree of tension, if not conflict. If the reformulation is to proceed from "within Christian faith and tradition," then how is one to know if the other religious traditions are being distorted or not? After all, the purpose is to avoid misconceptions and misinterpretations of other religions. For instance, how do theologians know what is offending or where it is hurting Hindus or Moslems, if they do not consult them? Finally, any reformulation must be intelligible *both* to Christians *and* to the followers of other faiths to whom it is being related. In other words, it cannot be done on a basis that is unintelligible to non-Christians either. Otherwise, we will end up in theological monologue. Basically, the point that Professor Dawe makes that there should be no "distortion" of other religions is valid. But how can it be ensured? It seems to me that the best way is to bring the "spirit" of Christianity, which is love, into operation in the Christian relations with other religions, cultures, and worldviews.

Following his guidelines, Professor Dawe rejects:

1. rationalistic humanism as a basis for dialogue, because it distorts Christianity as well as other religions;
2. modern secularity, because it is indifferent to religious particularity and itself has provided no adequate basis for world community;
3. Christian triumphalism, because it represents a distorted and demonic form of the Christian claim to finality.

First, I agree with his rejection of rationalistic humanism, although I believe that it has played a great role in bringing sanity into inter-religious relationships. But I do reject rationalistic humanism if it places reason above revelation or ignores revelation altogether. Second, the term "secularity" or "secularism" is as ambiguous as the word "religion" itself. Secularism, in the sense of absence of "official" religion, is conducive to religious freedom to practice and propagate the religious faith of one's choice. It is an important spiritual value. It is in this sense, for example, that the concept of secularism is understood in India. In the West, it is used in the sense of indifference to divine revelation. Professor Dawe rejects modern secularity in the western sense of the term. Third, he rejects Christian triumphalism as it represents a demonic form of particularity.

Professor Dawe uses the "covenant" concept to bring into relief the particularity and universality of Christianity. He uses it as a viable basis for relating Christian faith to other religious traditions, though there are several other concepts that may also be explored advantageously, like the "Cross," "kingdom of God," "Holy Spirit," and so forth. By a historical investigation and thorough consideration of the covenant concept, he distinguishes between an improper and exclusive interpretation and a proper and a universal interpretation of it. He shows that the covenant tradition expresses God's concern for all humanity. It also reveals the universality of God's sovereignty. On the basis of "radical monotheism," which says that "God is the God of all," he affirms that:

1. God's presence may be actualized through many traditions.
2. God is not ultimately known as "my God" or "our God"; he is not simply known as "the God of Abraham, Isaac, and Jacob," but as "Yahweh," the transcendent one.
3. Where human life is being fulfilled, it is a sign of the presence of God.
4. Christians may affirm the legitimacy of responses to God through religious traditions other than their own.
5. But to the Christians, the fullest disclosure of the relationship of God to the fulfillment of human existence is given in Jesus.

I am grateful for these affirmations. They take the sting out of Christian exclusivism. I fully respect and accept the fifth as a declaration of the Christian position.

In the context of these affirmations, Professor Dawe raises the question: What is to be made of the claim that other than

Jesus Christ "there is no other name under heaven given among men by which we must be saved." He also supplies an answer: The universality of Christianity is grounded in the translatability of the "name of Jesus," not in the imposition of particular formularies on others:

1. The "name of Jesus" is the encoding of the motif of death and resurrection as the key to the new being. This pattern is encountered in many religious traditions.
2. The worship due to him is the willingness to accept dying to the self as the way to life.
3. The finality of Jesus Christ is in the unconditioned way in which he points beyond himself, even to the point of surrendering his selfhood, so that humankind may find healing in the Unconditioned.

The *Rigveda* declares: "Truth is one; the sages call it by different names." It is not this or that cultic name, but the truth or meaning that is signified by the name that is crucial. Jesus signifies Cross, the dying to the self as the way to life. Hindus would say that the transcendence of the ego is the whole purpose of morality and spirituality. Enlightened persons gain release by the surrender of their little selves and their vanities, by purity of life and devotion to God.

The chief problem facing us today is the reconciliation of humankind. The religious traditions of the world are challenged to apply their resources to the resolution of the problem. History poses challenges, and if we restate our old principles in new ways, it is not because we will to do so, but because we must. Such a restatement of the truths of eternity in the accents of our times is the only way in which a great tradition or Scripture can be of living value. Professor Dawe's presentation illustrates Christian dynamism and creativity in the face of contemporary problems.

HINDU APPROACH

Reverence for the faith of other people has been an essential element in the Hindu spiritual vision. The Hindu tradition respects all prophets and sages who have come to guide humanity. Hindus have tried to give expression to an ecumenical spirit in religious matters. They believe that all the great religions of the world are not only relevant but also necessary in the context of the diversity of human needs. Each of them addresses a felt need in the spiritual progress of humanity. They hold that, at its deepest and best, each religious tradition constitutes a precious part of the religious heritage of humanity. They do not wish any religious tradition to compromise or capitulate. They wish all peoples to maintain the identity of respective symbols. They appreciate various forms of sincere worship and are willing to learn from other traditions.

The Hindu tradition justifies religious pluralism on the basis of *adhikara* (spiritual competence) and *istadevata* (chosen form of Deity). Different sects and traditions cater to a diversity of temperament and capacity. Accordingly, one and the same path is not recommended to all persons. The *Bhagavad Gita* teaches that one's faith is determined by one's *guna* (quality) and *karma* (action). Some religious insights and practices make sense to some persons, while others appeal to other personality types.

There are important differences as well as similarities between religious traditions. Since differences are important, and in some cases unbridgeable, no uncritical syncretism *(dharma sankara)* is acceptable, nor does the tradition advocate an undifferentiated universalism or easy indifferentism. While marvelling at the uniqueness of each religious tradition, Hindus appreciate the enrichment that comes from the religions being different. Each tradition is valued for the *differences* it brings to the human community. It makes Hindus humble and prevents a sense of complacency and self-sufficiency in their own beliefs.

The great Hindu teachers claim that religious differences cannot be understood in their true perspective until we appreciate the similarities among the traditions. By focusing on the resemblances, we are able to see human religiousness in its varied forms as opposed to a purely secular approach to life. While dogmatic differences separate religions, the inculcation of moral and spiritual values brings all of them together. The "Golden Rule" in one form or the other and the injunction to transcend egoism are present in all of them. When we wish to grow in partnership, we should appreciate the differences and work for a healthy harmony *(samavaya)* on the basis of possible agreements.

Hindu *dharma* is a philosophy and a way of life to guide people in moral and spiritual matters. It is not a religion in the usual sense of the term. Lord Krishna in the *Bhagavad Gita* asks Arjuna to give up all religions and seek refuge in Him. Affirmations such as *sattyannasti paro dharmah* ("there is no *dharma* higher than truth") and *ahimsa paramo dharmah* ("nonviolence is the highest virtue") give the basis for the regulation of Hindu life and conduct. Mahatma Gandhi described Hinduism as "a search for Truth through nonviolent means."

Hindus look upon the world as *dharmakshetra*, the field of moral and spiritual endeavors. *Dharma* assures wordly excellence and spiritual welfare of people as people, irrespective of all other conditions. Therefore, Hindus seek to support the moral and spiritual endeavors of the peoples all over the world.

Hindu *dharma* is based on certain enduring principles: the unity of Being *(advaita)*, search for Truth *(jijnasa)*, reverence for life *(ahimsa)*, spiritual discipline *(yoga)*, and the obligations to nature *(yajna)* and society *(dana)*. All these have enormous implications for world community. The unity of Being implies that all things in the universe are knit together in that which is the common basis of all existence. Spirituality probes this underlying unity of life and aims at universal well-being. It gives the philosophical root of nonviolence or love. It encourages a way of life where the individual is enabled to live in tune with the infinite. It seeks to turn neighborhood into brotherhood and society into community, in which all human beings are looked upon with love and kindliness. It asks people to transcend the barriers that their little egos have erected around themselves.

Hindu Scriptures, especially the *Upanishads*, reveal the unity of existence in *atman*, the self as universal soul or essence. They illustrate their conclusions with whatever positive knowledge was available when they were written. In recent centuries scientific knowledge has been advanced radically and vastly by modern science. It has yielded vast power resulting in the unprecedented advancement of some nations. But it has not necessarily brought peace, joy, mutual sharing, and fulfillment. Scientific advancement has been divorced from spiritual progress. Hindu *dharma* stresses the need to spiritualize science, so that the spirituality of science and the spirituality of religions could flow as a united stream to fertilize human life and create a happy and prosperous world community. World religions have a great role to play in humanizing science and technology.

The Hindu ideal presents a way of life geared to produce internal equilibrium and external harmony. Human life is plagued by the conflict between the divine and the demonic. This inner conflict is the basis of external disharmonies. To overcome this conflict and integrate personality is the aim of *yoga*. The Hindu tradition does not see *yoga* in competition with any religious tradition. Rather it helps a Hindu to become a better Hindu, a Christian a better Christian, and so forth. The central message of *yoga* is that the true self is liberated and united with God only when we have completely freed ourselves from all selfish attachment. Thinkers of other faiths have testified that their own dormant faith has come alive as a consequence of the practice of *yoga*.

HINDU VIEW OF CHRIST

Jesus Christ is an ineradicable part of modern Hinduism. Many Hindus adore Christ. The saving power of the Cross is felt in the lives of many Hindus in all walks of life. The way in which Christ has touched their lives and their response to him are varied: Some Hindus acknowledge Jesus as an *avatar*, others consider him as an *advaitin*, and still others understand him as a *yogi*, a *sulguru*, and so on. Mahatma Gandhi and Neo-Vedantins, for instance, show great reverence to Jesus Christ, but refuse exclusive devotion to him. Persons like Subba Rao are exclusively devoted to Christ, but stand within Hindu tradition.

Hindus do not accept that the Bible is the only Scripture and Jesus Christ is the only instance of God's self-disclosure. Christian arguments based on biblical authority or the authority of church fathers are not compelling to Hindus. And yet the Hindus accept the Bible, the Qur'an, and the Scriptures of other religions, along with the Vedas, as the Word of God. Here is a basic difference between Hindu and Christian approaches. Our purpose in dialogue should not be to eliminate differences, but to appreciate each other's faith, and cooperate with one another in overcoming violence, war, injustice, and irreligion in the world. In this regard, the following verses of the New Testament are very instructive:

And John answered and said, Master, we saw one casting out devils in thy name; and we forbade him because he followeth not with us. And Jesus said unto him, Forbid him not: for he that is not against us is for us [Luke 9:49–50].

There are many devils to be cast out. World religions should come together to vanquish them, *before* they destroy human community completely.

NOTE

1. S. Radhakrishnan, *Religion and Culture* (Delhi: Hind Pocket Books, 1968).

4

A Jewish Response:

The Lure and Limits of Universalizing Our Faith

Eugene B. Borowitz

Traditional Judaism has a reasonably well defined attitude to non-Jewish religions. The Torah describes God as making a covenant with Noah and thus, through Noah and his children, with all of humanity. The rabbis made this covenant the basis of their authoritative rulings about the religious status of non-Jews. They and all the Judaism that flowed from them considered the covenant with Noah to be real and continuing. Rabbinic Judaism thus believes all people know what God wants of them and can achieve their salvation. But as the Torah story of Noah immediately makes clear, humankind regularly violates its covenant responsibilities to God. The rabbis generally believed that the children of Noah were obligated to carry out seven root commandments: not to blaspheme God, or worship idols, or murder, or steal, or be sexually degenerate, or cut limbs from living animals, and, positively, to set up courts of justice. Even as the descendents of Noah built a tower to enter heaven and gain a name, so the rabbis saw most of humanity behaving sinfully and thus deserving of God's judgment.

The Torah understands the covenant with Abraham as a compensation for the sinfulness of humanity. The covenant with Noah is not abrogated by God. Rather God establishes a special covenant so that the divine rule may be properly established among people. Covenant being essentially a relationship of obligation, the Jews fulfill God's special purpose by living in special intensity under God's law. They proclaim the reality of God's rule by doing the commandments, personally and communally; by example, they set a standard for humanity.

Proselytizing has little role in Judaism. People do not need to be Jews; they need only be pious Noachides. So the Jews have no command to convert anyone. They do accept converts and, in love of their faith, occasionally seek to have others adopt it. The rabbis acknowledged that unconverted individuals among "the nations" could be fully righteous and thus "saved." The comment, "The pious among the gentiles have a share in the life of the world to come," may be taken as the standard Jewish attitude. The rabbis, like the Bible, were, however, spiritually pessimistic about human collectives and freely speculated that they would not survive the post-messianic judgment day. In our own time, the experience of the Holocaust, perpetrated by a nation steeped in Christianity and a leader of modern culture, has reinforced those traditional attitudes. While still hopeful about individuals we are skeptical if not cynical about claims for the goodness of human nature, the progress of civilization, or the way institutions will transform humanity. If I forebear from discussing the Holocaust further it is because I take it for granted that its horrifying reality is a motive for and an assumption of our discussion of world inter-religious relationships.

Yet for all this doctrine, the only gentile religion the rabbis directly dealt with was idolatry. Succeeding generations have had to fill in Judaism's judgment of other religions. With regard to Christianity this involved a consideration of whether it was not another form of idol worship. Its use of icons, its veneration of saints, and particularly its doctrine of the Christ as a person of the triune God, seemed the equivalent of idolatry. The slow development of a relatively positive assessment of Christianity has been beautifully traced by Jacob

Katz in his *Exclusiveness and Tolerance* and needs no further
statement here.[1] Islam being radically monotheistic caused
many fewer problems. Most Jewish thinkers today see pious
Christians and Muslims as fulfilling the Noachian covenant,
and thus as "saved." A minority opinion remains that their
worship is the equivalent of idolatry; also some modern Jews
have tried to give these religions a more than Noachian status,
in line with their own claims, but no such view has gained
even substantial minority support. This is as far as the Jewish
theory of other religions has gone. In sum, humanity does not
need to be Jewish but God needs Jews and Judaism to achieve
the divine purposes with humanity. This sense of the Jews as
chosen and special but only instrumental to the establishment
of God's kingdom is so great that some rabbis can see the
ultimate disappearance of Jewish distinctiveness at the conclusion of the eschatological drama, though most love the
Jewish people too much to believe that God would do without
them, even in the life of the world to come.

All this is, essentially, early rabbinic teaching. I find it remarkable how much of its nontriumphal universality Professor Dawe accepts and I cannot repress a Jewish sigh that it has
taken so many painful centuries for Christian thinkers to do
so.

I also think most believing Jews would find quite congenial,
as I do, Professor Dawe's method for potentially accepting the
religious legitimacy of many faiths. He does this as a matter of
Christian faith and not as a matter of enlightenment universalism or secularist pragmatism. He does consider it critical to
recognize that the world is incurably pluralistic religiously, but
he does not argue as some have done that the multiplicity of
religions itself demonstrates that none of them is true and that
truth is more likely to be found in what they share. The logic of
such quick derivations from comparative data escapes me.
That there are many religions is, in itself, no basis for denying
the truth claim of any one of them. Moreover, to argue that
multiplicity demonstrates commonality is a simple contradiction in terms. Rather, to see unity when there is diversity
before one requires a transempirical standard. The nature of

that standard and its source are critical to our discussion. If the standard is open enough to reach out to most of humankind, one might end up with a fairly unrestricted relativism: "All religions or almost all religions are equally worthwhile." If, however, while recognizing that many religions might be true, one's standard of judgment discriminates between religions as being more true and less true, then one may find oneself denying the adequacy of certain peoples' faiths.

The origin of one's basis for asserting universality may have a great affect on its nature. Dawe is quite precise in this regard. He is a universalist, he contends, because he is a Christian. So I am a universalist because I am a Jew. Our specific, historic faiths teach the possibility that all people can know God. I do not know that all other faiths teach such a doctrine. Indeed, for many centuries it seems fair to say that Christianity itself did not. One of my concerns in the study of comparative religion is to know which particular faiths assert similar doctrines and what sort of standard of judgment they apply to other faiths.

In any case, without a particularistic grounding for universalism I do not see how it can arise. Since the history of religion is descriptive, it cannot move on to statements of what is real in all religions, or what is their essence, without becoming philosophy of religion. Since religious universality is not self-evident it would need some rational argument, most likely a compelling metaphysics or ontology, to establish it. I see nothing like that in the competitive pluralism of theories we call philosophy of religion today, though I remain open to the possibility that reason here comes to coincide with what I have been taught by revelation. My point is that if universality is grounded in particular faith it would seem odd that universality could ever fundamentally negate the truth of particularity for in so doing it would destroy its own legitimation.

This concern for particularism leads me to raise some Jewish problems with Dawe's discussion of Christian universalism. I do so conscious of the fact that his paper is an exercise in outreach and inclusiveness, not a full statement of his Christianity. I concede that the timeliness and morality of his effort are not unimportant considerations. Nonetheless as all faiths move in a similar direction it is important to raise certain questions, essentially methodological ones. Coming to his universalism via Christianity, Professor Dawe has a standard by which to judge other faiths and says we cannot be undiscriminating. But being concerned to be inclusive he brings universalism to the brink of relativism. He gives us criteria for judging other faiths that are so broad—new being, human renewal, and fulfillment—that it is not clear what, if any, religious way of life might give him Christian pause. I suggest we shall not know whether Professor Dawe is not effectively a relativist until he tells us who he might conceivably exclude from his company of equivalent faiths.

The Jewish standard for such judgment is the Noachian covenant and one asks whether a given religion, in fact, reflects it. Thus one of the major problems that would arise in Jewish discussions with other faiths, Islam most notably excluded, is idol worship. This being the root sin to Judaism, strict authorities would allow for no efforts to explain away the facts of the practice. Lenient authorities might conceivably seek some mitigation on this point, even as in the case of Christianity, the identification of God with a human being, once considered the equivalent of idolatry, was no longer so understood. Another matter of major Jewish concern would be the attitude toward and the practice of the rules of conduct taken to be part of the Noachian covenant. A religion that did not make them central would not, from the Jewish view, be a proper way for humanity to serve God.

Dawe's elaboration of his criterion raises major problems for me with regard to theological method. His argument rests on an interpretation of Christianity as proclaiming the name of God as the name of Jesus. His own universalizing translation of that name is justified by the flat assertion: "This is true because the 'name of Jesus' is the disclosure of the structure of new being." How does he know that this is what the Christ really means and apparently has always meant? I do not recall such language in the New Testament or in medieval statements about the nature and work of the Christ. Rather it seems reasonably clear to me that Dawe is presenting us with one of the most appealing modern interpretations of the Christ, a personalist or existentialist one of a decided Tillichian flavor. He equates all of Christian tradition with this modern interpretation of it. I wonder. We know a good deal about the rise and fall of theological systems, of the ephemeral character of modern hermeneutics of the old great symbols, and, equally, of the present pluralism among Christian interpreters of the Christ. Why Dawe wants such a view of the Christ I find commendable, but it is not clear to me how, from within the circle of Christian faith, he arrives at his equation of Christianity and humanization. Despite his summoning of key symbols I cannot tell to what extent this is a reasonable reinterpretation of Christianity. This issue is common to many faiths today: How much modernization can an old tradition admit and still be true to itself. In contemporary Judaism, for example, many of our most significant arguments rage over how much one may change the concept or practice of Torah, or the extent to which Zionism is a full translation of classic Jewish identity.

What is more troubling to me, however, is Dawe's full-scale universalization of the truth of symbols that traditionally were as true in their particularity as in their universality. Let me give two examples. Dawe turns the Bible's God into a radically monotheistic Lord. If radical meant that there was only one God and that God was *Adonai,* we would have no argument. But for Dawe radical monotheism means more than absolute sovereignty. It means that God is so universally Lord that God cannot really be connected intimately with particulars. Radical monotheism is thus a "Protestant principle" that denies particular divine covenants. But the Bible knows no universal God who does not at the same time radically participate in the election and chosenness of particular covenant partners.

With regard to the Christ, Professor Dawe is more circumspect. He does not deny that Jesus of Nazareth was a particular man of a given historical locus, and he does not denigrate the fact that a particular group of people, Christians, see in this individual, "the fullest disclosure of the relationship of God to the fulfillment of human existence." But when done translating Christhood into humanization, no particular truth, no special claim attaches to Jesus, the Christ, or to Christians. Instead, again and again we hear that wherever new being generates human fulfillment, wherever life is renewed and virtue expressed, one has the equivalent of the Christian's Christ. Thus, such truth as Christianity has is universal. What is particular about Christianity has been relegated to a second, perhaps valuable, but certainly not essential, level of truth and value.

On what basis is this done? Professor Dawe said he would speak from a Christian base. But Christianity itself has not previously authorized this emptying out of its particularity. Perhaps the issue is better put in logical terms: How does he know that particularist symbols can be fully translated into universalistic terms? In the fact of previous failures to de-particularize Christianity and show it as essentially universal truth, how does Dawe now validate this method and these results?

Perhaps it will be helpful to set these questions in a sociological framework, though I know I now border on the impolite. For which Christians does this sort of universalism speak? And what does Dawe think of the Christian legitimacy of those who will differ with him? Answering the same about myself, I am a Reform Jew whose liberalism is uncommonly traditional. Many Reform and some Conservative Jews would be far less particularistic than I am. At the other extreme few if any Orthodox Jewish thinkers would find congenial the sort of discussion of faith being engaged in here. The Jewish community, as a whole, I suggest is increasingly committed to the proposition that Judaism's symbols, while bearing high universalistic import, cannot fully be rendered in universal terms. From late in the nineteenth century to our own time, Jews have lived with the effort to translate Torah into simple human ethics. This produced some strikingly positive results in terms of Jewish contributions to the welfare of humankind. It also laid the intellectual foundations for generations of unconcern with Jewish identity and belief. Now we are beginning to see the cumulative effect of this denial of our roots: With the erosion of our particularism our ethical commitments have now also begun to slip. Our non-believing Jews—a high proportion of our community—do not seem to care much about this. I obviously do not speak for them. For most of the rest of us, seeing what has happened to our people's conduct has ended the quest for articulating Judaism as universalism in these pre-messianic times.

I suppose my ultimate objection to Dawe's method is its apparent consequences. To humanize Christianity he has made it dispensable. Jews, not acknowledging the occurrence of a messianic resurrection in history, take the potential death of a covenant partner more seriously. I wonder if Professor Dawe would object if his children adopted humanizing, non-Christian faiths, married their adherents, and raised his grandchildren in them? To his mind, would there be any *theological* loss if Christianity should disappear as an identifiable religion? Or would it mean the loss of merely another socio-cultural humanizing faith? We Jews are much more particularistic than that. We want our children to be Jews and marry Jews so there can be Jewish homes so that Jewish people and its faith can survive, set an example of covenant faithfulness, and ultimately give birth to the Messiah. Paradoxically enough even those rabbis who justify performing intermarriages generally do so as helping to keep the family and its children within the Jewish community! Our concern for particularity goes that far.

This leaves Jews, and I think all major religious traditions, with a perplexing methodological problem. Contemporary western intellectuality has no good contexts for validating particularity. A proper explanation or proof always involves relation to a universal rule or truth. Individuality is significant only as an instance of a class or category. It has the worth of a necessary accident, finitude being our lot, though it may also have instrumental value. As soon as one seeks to raise particularity above this level one must have recourse to generally denigrated patterns of legitimation. One can utilize terms like "revelation," "tradition," "dogma," "authority," or, more philosophically, "fideism." These have almost no persuasive power among sophisticated western university academicians.

Becoming a professor apparently commits one to universalize truth. Take the case of existentialism. Kierkegaard thought that he was validating truth as a particular, individual matter. Today we turn that into a general theory of what it is to be a person and existentialism is used, as in Dawe's case, to departicularize.

My Jewish faith leads me to assert that there is no inherent need to departicularize one's faith because one is drawn to its universal vision of humanity. I suggest that we may find it far more valuable and authentic to acknowledge our simultaneous assertion of particular and universal truths and see how we can envision our particularity so as not to violate our universality. This is not easy. The tension between the particular and the universal will always plague such a paradoxical faith as it does Judaism. And the human will to sinfulness and self-service being so great, chauvinism and fanaticism can easily blind us to our intimate involvement with all human beings.

Our particularism may then need some special limits and I can suggest four that faiths might insist upon. First, we can limit the role of our particularity, applying it only to ourselves, as in the Jewish assertion that only Jews, not all people, need to serve God in the specifically Jewish way. Second, one may adopt the liberal religious stance and acknowledge that one's sense of religious truth, while great enough to stake one's life on, is not absolute. One must then allow room for others with a different sense of truth. Third, whether one can accept the liberal stance or not, one may recognize that religion today stands under the moral judgment of its secular critics. For pragmatic reasons, then, we must not act so as to discredit our claims to serve a universal God. Such a concern for what others think would undoubtedly change as we found ourselves in a position of power, precisely when we need the greatest restraint. Perhaps then, fourth, we can admit that the fullness of the truth we affirm can come into being only in God's eschatological redemption of all human history. Until then we must do our share while recognizing that we ourselves stand under God's present judgment and must leave to

God what God alone can do. In fact, as a liberal Jew, I believe all four of these theses. This does not resolve the paradox of my simultaneous Jewish particularism and universalism or relieve me of the need in each decision not to transgress against either of my commitments. But paradox is the sign of expulsion from Eden and only in the new Eden will it finally be taken from us.

NOTE

1. Jacob Katz, *Exclusiveness and Intolerance: Studies in Medieval and Modern Times* (London: Oxford University Press, 1961).

5

A Muslim Response:

Christian Particularity
and the Faith of Islam

Fazlur Rahman

Islam's attitude to Christianity is as old as Islam itself, since Islam partly took shape at the point of its very genesis by both adopting certain important ideas from Judaism and Christianity and criticizing others. Indeed, Islam's self-definition is partly the result of its attitude to these two religions and their communities.

That there was messianism present among certain Meccan Arab circles at the time Muhammad appeared is undeniable. This fact has been amply documented. And instead of accepting either Judaism or Christianity, these Arab circles were looking for a new revealed religion of their own, so that "they might be even better guided" than the two older communities. After the advent of Muhammad as God's messenger, the Qur'an (Koran)* repeatedly refers to a group of people about whom it says, "We had already given them the Book [i.e., the Torah and/or the Gospel] and they also believe in the Qur'an." These verses clearly show the existence of some Jews or Christians or Judeo-Christians who had also entertained messianic hopes and who encouraged Muhammad in his mission. The Qur'an, indeed, taunts the Meccan pagans saying that whether they believed or not in the Qur'an (or the Prophet),

---

* This essay uses transliterations from the Arabic for names instead of the more familiar, but often misleading, English forms of the names. Hence, Qur'an for Koran, Madina for Medina, and Muhammad for Mohammed.

"those to whom We had already given the Book, believe in it [or him]." [1]

There are several important and interesting issues connected with this phenomenon. For example, was Islam entirely the result of Jewish and/or Christian "influences," or was it basically an independent native growth that nevertheless picked up some important ideas from the Judeo-Christian tradition? A number of Jewish and Christian scholars have vied with each other to show that Islam was genetically related to the one or the other religion. Recently several western scholars, among them Montgomery Watt, Gaudefroy Demomlyness, and, above all, H.A.R. Gibb, have argued convincingly that in its nativity Islam grew out of an Arab background, although in its formation and development there have been many important influxes of the Judeo-Christian tradition. [2] But the issue with which we are directly concerned here is not of the "originality" of Islam but with Muhammad's perception of himself and his mission, which is intimately connected with his perception of his relationship to other prophets, their religion(s), and their communities.

It is quite obvious from the Qur'an that from the beginning to the end of his prophetic career Muhammad was absolutely convinced of the divine character of the earlier revealed documents and of the divine messengership of the bearers of these documents. This is the reason why he recognized without a moment of hesitation that Abraham, Moses, Jesus, and other Old and New Testament religious personalities had been genuine prophets like himself. This acceptance was undoubtedly strengthened by the recognition on the part of some followers of these earlier religions of Muhammad as a true prophet and of the Qur'an as a revealed book. Hence the falsity of the view popular among western Islamists (originally enunciated by the patriarchs of western Islamic studies like Snouck Hurgrange and Noeldehe Schwally) that in Mecca the Prophet Muhammad was fully convinced that *he was giving to the Arabs* what Moses and Jesus *had previously given to their respective communities,* and that it was at Madina, where the Jews refused to recognize him as God's messenger, that he instituted the Muslim community as separate from Jews and Christians. [3]

There is, indeed, no trace of any fixed religious communities in the earlier part of the Qur'an. True, different prophets have come to different peoples and nations at different times, but their messages are universal and identical. All these messages emanate from a single source: "the Mother of the Book" (VIII, 4) and "the Hidden Book" (LVI, 78). Since these messages are universal and identical, it is incumbent on all people to believe in all divine messages. This is the reason why Muhammad felt himself obligated to believe in the prophethood of Noah, Abraham, Moses, and Jesus, since God's religion is indivisible and prophethood is also indivisible. Indeed, the Prophet is made to declare in the Qur'an that not only does he believe in the Torah and the Gospel but "I believe in whatever Book God may have revealed" (XLII, 15). This is because God's guidance is universal and not restricted to any nation or nations: "And there is no nation wherein a warner has not come" (XXXV, 24) and "for every people a guide has been provided" (XIII, 7). The word "Book" is, in fact, often used in the Qur'an not with reference to any specific revealed book but as a generic term denoting the totality of divine revelations (see II, 213, for example).

If Muhammad and his followers believe in all prophets, all people must also and equally believe in him. Disbelief in him would be equivalent to disbelief in all, for this would arbitrarily upset the line of prophetic succession. In the late Meccan period, however, the Prophet becomes more aware that Jews and Christians would not believe in him, nor would they recognize each other. Recent scholarship has shown that this awareness came to Muhammad in Mecca and not in Madina, as often believed. At this point, Jews and Christians are called *al-ahzab* (sectarians, partisans, people who are divisive of the unity of religion and disruptive of the line of prophetic succession), each *hizb* (also *shi'a*) or party rejoicing in what it has to the exclusion of the rest. Muslims are warned not to split up into parties. It is at this point that the religion of Muhammad is described as "straight" and "upright," the religion of the *hanif* (i.e., of an upright monotheist who does not follow divisive forces) and is linked and identified with the religion of Abraham.

In both these verses, the vast majority of Muslim commentators exercise themselves fruitlessly to avoid having to admit the obvious meaning, viz., that those who believe in God and the Last Day and do good deeds—from any section of humankind—are saved. They either say that by Jews, Christians, and Sabaeans here are meant those who have actually become "Muslims"—which interpretation is clearly belied by the fact that "Muslims" constitute the first of the four groups mentioned, i.e., "those who believe"—or that they were those good Jews, Christians, and Sabaeans who lived before the advent of the Prophet Muhammad—which is an even worse *tour de force.* Even when replying to Jewish and Christian claims that the hereafter was theirs and theirs alone, the Qur'an says, "On the contrary, whosoever surrenders himself to God while he does good deeds as well, he shall find his reward with his Lord, shall have no fear, nor shall he come to grief" (II, 112).

The logic of this recognition of universal goodness, with belief in one God and the Last Day as its necessary basis or underpinning, demands, of course, that the Muslim community be recognized as *a* community among communities. Here, the Qur'an appears to give its final answer to the problem of a multi-community world when the subject is treated in V, 48:

And We have sent down to you the Book in truth, confirming the Book that existed already before it and protecting it. . . . For each one of you [several communities] We have appointed a Law and a Way of Conduct [while the essence of religion is identical]. If God had so willed, He would have made all of you one community, but [He has not done so] that He may test you in what He has given you; *so compete in goodness.* To God shall you all return and He will tell you [the Truth] about what you have been disputing.

The positive value of different religions and communities, then, is that they may compete with each other in goodness (cf. II, 148, 177, where, after announcing the change in the *Qibla*—direction of prayer—from Jerusalem to Mecca, it is emphasized that the *Qibla* per se is of no importance, the real worth being in virtue and *competing in goodness*). The Muslim community itself, lauded as the "Median Community" (II,144) and "the best community produced for mankind" (III, 110), is given no assurance whatever that it will be automatically God's darling unless it, when it gets power on the earth, establishes prayers, provides welfare for the poor, commands good, and prohibits evil (XXII, 41, etc.). In XLVII, 38, the Muslims are warned that "if you turn your backs [upon this teaching], God will substitute another people for you who will not be like you" (cf. IX, 38).

In the light of the foregoing considerations, it is, therefore, a welcome development that Professor Dawe has attempted to interpret the Christian dogma more positively to extend the possibility of salvation outside the Christian church. This is especially welcome in view of what he calls "Christian triumphalism," which had earned particular odium because of its alliance with western colonialism in the eighteenth, nineteenth, and twentieth centuries to which it was often a junior partner. So far as Islam is concerned, it recognized Jesus and his divine mission from the time of its birth. However, it criticized, sometimes severely, the doctrine of the incarnation of God in Jesus and, consequently, rejected trinitarianism. Christians have mostly taken this to be a rejection of Christianity itself. The Qur'an assigns to Jesus the position of a prophet, God's Word and Divine Spirit, but withholds—for reasons that are not arbitrary or fortuitous but rooted deeply in its very conception of the God-human relationship—assent to the divinity of Jesus or, indeed, of anybody else.

According to the Qur'an, the most fundamental distinction between God and creatures is that God is infinite—All-Life, All-Power, All-Knowledge, etc.—whereas all creatures are finite. God, the Infinite, has created everything "according to a measure" (e.g., LIV, 49). He alone is the "Measurer *(Qadir)*," while everything else is "measured *(maqdur)*." This idea is, indeed, ubiquitous in the Qur'an. This is not a doctrine of "pre-determinism," as many Muslim theologians of the medieval ages understood it to be. "Measuring" in this context simply means "finitude" of potentialities, despite their range. Human beings, for example, are acknowledged by the Qur'an to be possessed of great potentialities: Adam outstripped angels in a competition of creative knowledge and angels were thus ordered to honor him (II, 30 ff.); yet human beings cannot be God.

It is because of the infinitude of God that both absolute mercy and absolute power are equally attributable to God alone. God's mercy is literally limitless (L, 7; VII, 156)—indeed, mercy is a law written into God's nature (VI, 12). And the very fact that there exists the plenitude of being rather than the emptiness of nonbeing is an expression of the primal act of God's mercy. God's power is commensurate with God's mercy. You may not point to any human being, with delimitations and a date of birth, and say simply "that person is God." To the Qur'an, this is neither possible, nor intelligible, nor pardonable.

The severity of the Qur'an's judgments on incarnation and trinity has varied. There are verses that regard the Christian doctrine simply as "extremism in faith":

O People of the Book! do not go to extremes in your faith and do not say about God except truth. The Messiah, Jesus, son of Mary was but a Messenger of God and His Word that He cast into Mary and a spirit from Him. So believe in God and in His Messengers and say not "[God] is there," desist from this, it is better for you. God is but one and only God—far above He be from having a son; to Him belong whatever is in the heaven and in the earth. . . . The Messiah [Jesus] will not be too proud to be God's servant, nor will those angels who are very near God [disdain to be His servants]. And whosoever should disdain to do service to Him and be too proud [for this], God will gather all of them to Himself [on the Last Day] (II, 171–72; cf. V, 77).

But there are much stronger verses reminiscent of the Qur'anic statements against idolators:

Those are infidels who say "God is the Messiah, son of Mary." Say "Who will be of any help against God, if He should want to destroy the Messiah, son of Mary, his mother and all those who live on the earth? To God belongs the kingdom of the heaven and the earth and whatever is between them; He creates whatever He wills, and God is powerful over everything" (V, 117).

Again,

Committed to infidelity are those who say "God is the same as the Messiah, son of Mary"; . . . committed to infidelity are those who say "God is one among three"—while there is no God but the Unique one—; if they do not desist from what they say, a painful punishment will touch those of them as commit infidelity. Why do they not repent to God and seek His pardon, for God is forgiving and merciful? The Messiah, son of Mary, was but a Messenger—before him had gone many other messengers; his mother was the truthful one; they both used to eat food [like other men]. Just see how We make the signs clear to them and also see how they are being deceived! (V, 72–75).

The Qur'an speaks in the same vein about and to Muhammad:

Muhammad is but a Messenger—before him have gone many other Messengers. Should he then die or be slain [in battle] will you turn back upon your heels [O Muslims!]? (III, 144).

Say [to the pagan Arabs], "Tell me, if God were to destroy me and all those who are with me, or should have mercy upon us, who will provide refuge . . . ?" (LXVII, 28).

Muhammad cannot take it for granted that God will automatically continue to send him revelatory messages:

Do they say that he [Muhammad] concocts lies and attributes them to God? But if God so will, He may seal up your heart [O Muhammad! so that no revealed message will issue forth from it]—indeed, God [not Muhammad] obliterates the falsehood and confirms what is true, through His Words . . . (XLII, 24).

For the Qur'an, then, Jesus can be as little an incarnation of God as Muhammad himself or, indeed, any other prophet. But it is true that the Qur'an speaks with tenderness of Jesus and also his followers (see V, 82: "You shall find the nearest of all people in friendship to the Believers [i.e., 'Muslims'] those who say they are Christians. This is because among them there are priests and monks and they are not a proud people"; also LVII, 27: "Then we followed up [these Messengers] with

Jesus, son of Mary, to whom We gave the Evangel, and We put in the hearts of his followers kindness and mercy . . . ''). This attitude toward Christianity has no parallel toward other communities mentioned in the Qur'an. Because the Qur'an is sometimes very mild, indeed, highly tender toward Christians (although at times it is highly critical of Christians), some western scholars have thought that basically Muhammad was a fellow-traveler and perhaps almost a Christian. It has been argued that political motivations prevented him from a full and explicit identification with Christianity. Some have also seen his increasing hostility toward Byzantium as the cause of the increasingly severe criticism of Christianity in the Qur'an. Some also think that he didn't correctly understand the nature of the doctrine of Jesus in Christianity, for it was misrepresented to him by Christians. On the latter, it is difficult to see how the doctrine of incarnation, for example, could be misunderstood. The trouble with the first view is that it is impossible to prove that the severely critical passages of the Qur'an are necessarily later than other passages. For example, LVII, 27, seems to be quite late Madinan. The truth, then, appears to be that Muhammad must have encountered various views at the hands of various representatives of Christianity and that the Qur'an appears to address different groups at different points.

In any case, the unacceptability of Jesus' divinity and the Trinity to the Qur'an is an incontrovertible fact, as is the fact that Jesus and his followers are regarded as exceptionally charitable and self-sacrificing. The Qur'an would most probably have no objection to the Logos having become flesh if the Logos were not simply identified with God and the identification were understood less literally. For the Qur'an, the Word of God is never identified simply with God. Jesus, again, is the ''Spirit of God'' in a special sense for the Qur'an, although God had breathed His spirit into Adam as well (XV, 29; XXXVIII, 72). It was on the basis of some such expectations from the self-proclaimed monotheism of Christians—and, of course, Jews—that the Qur'an issued its invitation: ''O People of the Book! Let us come together upon a formula which is common between us—that we shall not serve anyone but

God, that we shall associate none with Him . . . '' (III, 64). This invitation, probably issued at a time when Muhammad thought not all was yet lost between the three self-proclaimed monotheistic communities, must have appeared specious to Christians. It has remained unheeded until now. But I believe something can be still worked out by way of positive cooperation provided the Muslims hearken more to the Qur'an than to the historic formulations of Islam and provided that the pioneering efforts like that of Professor Dawe continue to yield a Christian doctrine more compatible with universal monotheism and egalitarianism.

NOTES

1. For a fuller discussion of these points, see my article ''Pre-Foundations of the Muslim Community in Mecca,'' in *Studia Islamica,* June 1976.

2. W. Montgomery Watt, *Muhammad at Mecca* (Oxford: Clarendon Press, 1953), pp. 1–29; Maurice Gaudefroy-Demomlyness, *Mahomet* (Paris: A. Michel, 1957), pp. i–xxii; and H.A.R.Gibb, ''Pre-Islamic Monotheism in Arabia,'' *Harvard Theological Review* 55 (1962). 269–80.

3. See my article ''Pre-Foundations of the Muslim Community in Mecca.''

PART TWO

THE DIALOGUE
WITHIN CHRISTIANITY

6

Religion as a Problem for Christian Theology

John B. Carman

A CONVERSATION IN THE RAMAYAPATNAM CLINIC

I was waiting my turn in the modest equivalent to the University Health Services at the Baptist Seminary at Ramayapatnam in the Telugu-speaking state of Andhra Pradesh in South India. This clinic, however, was open not only to students and faculty, like myself, but also to people from the surrounding villages, including the once proud port that gave us our name, now shrunk to a mere fishing village. Just in front of me the elderly *pantalamma* (evangelist or "Bible woman") was talking to a younger woman from the village, trying to communicate the gospel of Jesus Christ to her, with considerable emphasis on the error of her non-Christian ways and the futility of "those idols you worship." At some point the evangelist was interrupted by two young men in the seminary, who like me were waiting to see the doctor on his weekly visit.

"No, no, you shouldn't talk that way anymore," they said to the Bible woman in the same tone of reproof she had used in speaking to the Hindu villager. "We are now being taught that it is wrong to criticize the religion of Hindus and Muslims. We must try to understand them and thus adapt the gospel to their needs." That is all I remember of that conversation. At the time I was more concerned with getting my turn with the doctor, which was the reason all of us, except the evangelist, were there. I remember that I was appalled by this multiple monologue and frustrated by my own inability to take part in it. I knew enough Telugu to understand the conversation but not enough to say anything—or at least that was the excuse for my silence.

You may be appalled for a different reason, appalled at the Christian evangelist pushing her version of the Christian message at one of the sick patients. But I was used to that mission institution of the "Bible woman," as she was commonly called. I believe that her direct approach to the spiritual needs of the patients in the clinic was at least as effective as the more sophisticated methods of U.S. hospital chaplains schooled in the teaching of Carl Rogers! Her basic message was about the divine love of the Lord Jesus, a love that was expressed through healing doctors and caring nurses as well as through the preaching evangelists, to transform the lives of every individual and family in the villages, even those living, as this villager did, in the separate hamlet for outcastes at the edge of the main village. Indeed, it was especially to these outcastes that the Christian church has for a century brought a practical gospel of liberation and transformation.

What I had overheard was not the whole story. But it was the negative approach to other religions that she had learned from one of my missionary predecessors, an approach that much of the Christian tradition has seen to be clearly present in the Bible, in both the Old Testament and the New.

What appalled me wasn't the negative tone of the Bible woman, but the equally negative tone of the students who interrupted her. They represented the new improved Christian approach—my approach, if you will—but the way that approach came across was just as negative as the old one. With the confidence of youth and the authority of superior learning they were telling the elderly evangelist what she was doing wrong, but they were not themselves relating to the Hindu woman. They had only interrupted the evangelist's conversation. Also, they gave the evangelist no clue as to how this new sympathetic approach was to deal with the sin in village religion, which for the evangelist and predecessors is summed up in the one word "idolatry." Now it may be that local custom prevented the young men from speaking directly to a woman; that is why, after all, we had women evangelists. But that explanation for noninvolvement was only a symptom of the larger human problem, just as was my inability to speak—to the seminary students, to the evangelist, or to the village woman. I had been so busy finishing my dissertation for a university ten thousand miles away that I had not had time to learn to communicate any version of the Christian message in the language of the people among whom I was living. For the seminary students and for me, the new approach was a negative tool to demonstrate some superior wisdom. It was not a wisdom that came to terms with the facts of village religion or that provided older Christians with some insightful alternative to what they regarded as the biblical denunciation of all idolatry.

In the thirteen years since this incident took place, I have been concerned with the comparative study of religion in a U.S. university context, and specifically with the Harvard Center for the Study of World Religions, where the Christian students and professors try to listen attentively to representatives of Eastern religions, certainly not to proselytize among them, unless to win them to the academic creed of sympathetic understanding! That stance has much to be said for it. Yet it may be that it has encouraged me to evade a problem that seemed of little interest for most people at Harvard, the problem that religion poses for Christian theology.

POSITIVE UTILIZATION OF THE CONCEPT OF RELIGION

There are many sides to this problem. I shall be able to touch on two of them: first, very briefly, on the *fact* of religious diversity and, second, on the modern western *concept* of religion.

The problem posed for Christian theology by the fact of religious diversity has been much discussed in recent years. But it is relatively new as a serious theological problem. Although Christianity has been one among many religions ever since its beginning as an irregular Jewish sect, for centuries many Christian communities took little notice of this fact. Nowhere was this blindness to meaningful religious diversity more striking than in medieval and early modern Western Europe. To be sure Western Christendom had boundaries, beyond which were the Muslim Turks, triumphant over the Christian armies of the Crusades and conquerors of much of Southeastern Europe: and within the geographical walls of Christendom were the Jews—an irritating exception to the unity of Christian society. With the expansion of Christianity after the sixteenth century, especially in the nineteenth and twentieth centuries, Christians have come to live alongside many more non-Christians in many more countries. Moreover, in many countries, including traditionally Christian societies that have undergone liberal or Marxist secularization, Christians are now self-consciously in a minority position.

While the problem of "other religions" becomes much more obvious for Christian theologians in this modern situation, there are still large parts of the Christian church in which this problem has hardly been discussed. Having Muslim or Hindu neighbors across the street does not by itself create a theological issue, let alone suggest a theological solution. Even in *western* Christianity, with its greater interest in abstract theological discussion, the discussions of "Christianity and other religions" has until recently been confined to the small fraction of Christian thinkers involved in the so-called "missionary enterprise." The theological giants of the previous generation generally had a rather superficial knowledge of other religions. Paul Tillich might seem to be an exception, but his trip to Japan and his subsequent book came at the very end of his life, long after his systematic theology had taken firm shape.

Yet while Christian theologians are only beginning to deal seriously with "other religions," they have for centuries been familiar with the concept of religion. It is the problems and opportunities associated with that concept that are my main concern here. The word "religion" has been in the Christian vocabulary for many centuries. The concept of religion became more familiar at the time of the Renaissance, the Protestant Reformation, and the Roman Catholic Counter Reformation. In the eighteenth century Enlightenment there was a striking development. Those rationalist thinkers opposed to the church came to view "natural religion" as distinct from and even opposed to organized Christianity. Those rationalist thinkers who continued to feel themselves part of the church, on the other hand, regarded a rationally purified Christianity as the highest form of religion, or even as the essence of religion in general.

The Protestant theologian who tried to wrest the new Enlightenment concept of religion from the hands of the church's critics was Friedrich Schleiermacher. He accepted the fact of a universal religious consciousness in human beings, but he rejected the notion of natural religion or of religion in general as something that actually exists. Actual religion, in his view, was necessarily particular. This is true even of his early, more romantic, defense of the religious consciousness. It is even more true of his later systematic statement of Christian faith. In Schleiermacher's later view, all human religion has its root in the feeling of absolute dependence. Christian piety is one particular form of human religion, that form in which *everything* is related to the mediation of Jesus Christ. Doctrines are not direct apprehensions of Divine Truth, whether pronounced in Scripture or revealed in nature, but human intellectual constructions making sense of the distinctively Christian form of the feeling of absolute dependence.

It should be quite clear that Schleiermacher did not intend to denigrate Christian faith by treating it as one species of a universal human genus, the genus of religion. He intended precisely to establish it as the highest form of piety, but to do so in a way that recognized other religions as positive expressions of the same common religious feeling. Those intentions continued among the more liberal Protestant theologians for the next hundred years. Some questioned whether the theological superiority of Christian religion could be determined on the basis of the contents of its distinctive religious feeling alone, or whether it depends on the joining of that religious feeling to a superior and distinctively Christian kind of ethical evaluation or moral judgment. Another and more modern alternative was enunciated by Ernst Troeltsch, for whom the forms of human religion were incomparable in magnitude. Thinkers who were Christians could do no more than affirm the truth of Christianity for those in the Christian community, or—at the most—those in western civilization.

At the very time Protestant theologians were either developing a position of religious relativism or rejecting the theologians' use of the concept of religion, Roman Catholic theology was making increasing use of the concept of religion. These more recent Catholic reflections continue a long tradition in seeing religion as ritual, whether sacramental rites, public and private prayer, or spiritual disciplines. The inner religious disposition is clearly important, too, but in contrast to the Protestant emphasis on inward piety, Roman Catholics have stressed the importance of ritual actions. It is not surprising that the twentieth-century Catholic counterparts to the nineteenth-century Protestant utilization of religion as a theological category should place more stress on universal human patterns of ritual observance. Within Catholic piety, it is fundamental that God's grace is mediated through the sacraments of the Catholic church. Once Catholic theologians have agreed that God also grants salvation to those outside of the visible church, it is only one step further to affirm that the divine grace making possible the salvation of non-Christians normally comes through the rituals of their own religious communities. Contemporary Roman Catholic theologians differ as to whether this saving reality in other religious systems was only in the past, as part of the preparation for the fulfillment of that sacramental reality in the Christian church, or is a present reality in at least some other religious systems. The position Karl Rahner takes in his article "Chrisitanity and Non-Christian Religions" is in between. "Christianity is the absolute and only religion determined for all mankind," but

until that moment when the gospel truly enters the historical situation of a given man, a non-Christian religion . . . includes not only elements of a natural knowledge of God intermingling elements of depravation due to human frailty flowing from original sin, but also supernatural moments of that grace which is given man by God on Christ's account, and therefore it can be acknowledged as a *legitimate* religion.[1]

Both the more and less radical proponents of this contemporary Roman Catholic view would agree that religion is an integral and valuable part of human nature and human society. Both Christianity and other religions are in their concrete institutional forms species, some lower and some higher, of the universal genus of religion. They also agree that these individual forms do not merely exist alongside one another, but that Christianity has been enriched by what converts bring into it of their previous religious life. For the more conservative theologians, the other religions are at some point superseded by the church and their values incorporated into the church. For the more radical thinkers, the "other religions" continue to be legitimate and valuable alternative expressions of religion, from which the church can be enriched in the present and future through the process of dialogue. Thus the other religions have not only a theoretical legitimacy for their own adherents, but also a practical value for the Christian community. At the least they have served as preparation for religious life within the church; at the most, they are the church's continuing teachers.

NEO-REFORMATION CHALLENGES TO THE CONCEPT OF RELIGION

For those unacquainted with Christian theology in this century, it may be something of a surprise to learn that much of Protestant thought since the First World War, instead of building on the nineteenth-century liberal Protestant notion of religion or interacting with the more positive twentieth-century Roman Catholic interpretations of non-Christian religions, has apparently repudiated both, as well as the notions of Christianity present in more conservative Protestant piety. These thinkers may have contributed to a reinforcement of traditional Christian exclusivism, but the points of view they develop, while drawing on the teachings of Luther and Calvin, are almost as critical of nineteenth-century Protestant orthodoxy as they are of Protestant liberalism and of Roman Catholic theology.

Fundamental to all these neo-Reformation interpretations is a sharp distinction between revelation, which is divine communication of what human beings could not discover for themselves, and religion, which is human activity to gain divine favor. Not only is there a sharp distinction between revelation and religion, but there is also a negative evaluation of religion, in one of three forms. The most radical is the thesis of "religionless" Christianity, familiar to many in the writing of Gogarten and A. T. van Leeuwen, which claims to be based on the insights recorded by Dietrich Bonhoeffer in his prison diary as well as the famous dictum of Karl Barth, *Religion ist Unglaube* ("Religion is lack of faith"). In this view the true form of Christian faith is devoid of religion and indeed in fundamental opposition to religion. From the time of the Hebrew prophets onward, true faith has shown its opposition to human religion, but now in our time it is possible to rid faith completely of the trappings of religion and proclaim a completely secular gospel for modern people.

This complete separation of religion and Christian faith is difficult to sustain and is much less significant for our topic than two other more complex approaches, each of which is in a different sense "dialectical," i.e., speaking both a Yes and No about the value of religion. One of these is the dialectical theology of Karl Barth, which because of the emphasis Barth himself puts on one side of the dialectic is usually understood in a most undialectical way. The title of the section in Barth's *Church Dogmatics* that deals with this question appears in English translation as "Revelation as the Abolition of Religion." The word translated as "abolition" is *Aufheben,* and this translation corresponds to normal modern usage. *Aufheben,* however, is not an ordinary word, but a central concept in the dialectical philosophy of Hegel, a philosophy of movement between Yes and No, not as simple oscillation but as spiral movement: from thesis to antithesis to synthesis.

Hegel took the word from a South German dialect (I think Schwäbisch), where it is used for the process of canning and preserving, and it is indeed an equivalent of our English expression, "putting something up." Is the housewife who turns fruits into preserves or cucumbers into pickles engaged essentially in preservation, abolition, or transformation? Whatever your metaphysical examination of a pickle jar may bring to light, the cook is in fact doing all three things. What makes this so important is that Hegel regards all human history, in every field of culture, as in a constant process of *aufheben*. Culture is constantly being "put up" or—if you prefer—"pickled," i.e., being so changed that it is in one sense destroyed, in another sense preserved, and in still another sense elevated to a higher level.

Barth does not say that he is using the term *Aufheben* in a specifically Hegelian sense. Yet it surprises me that Barth's disciples have generally not seen that this Hegelian term is the key to Barth's complicated interpretation of religion: Religion is a human reality that God destroys, preserves, and takes up to a higher level. Barth implies, it seems to me, that one can conceive of religion as a bare human possibility. This would be the Hegelian thesis. Most of Barth's emphasis, however, is on the Hegelian antithesis, namely that human beings make a mess of this human possibility, producing the very opposite to a positive relation to God, the creator. The final word about religion is positive—not, as in a Hegelian synthesis, because of the dynamic movement within the concept itself, but because of something outside the human possibility itself, the grace of God. God intervenes and takes those otherwise misused human religious forms and uses them as instruments of salvation. To be sure, in the way in which Barth develops this dialectic it is all religions that are involved in phase two (the antithesis) and only Christianity that is involved in phase three (the synthesis). But the problem of whether there should be a special place for Christian religion is a different question from the question of the significance of religion as such as a theological concept. On the one hand, Barth seems to be fighting against the basing of systematic theology on a general concept of religion, but, on the other hand, to be recognizing that there is a basic religious consciousness of human beings that serves as the arena in which the immensely consequential struggle between good and evil goes on.

A different and less ambiguous dialectical position is taken by a large number of European Protestant theologians, of whom the best known in this country is probably Hendrik Kraemer. One of Kraemer's colleagues at the University of Leiden, Prof. F. W. A. Korff, put that view as follows: Human beings are always addressed by God and also answer God. That answer is both positive and negative. Korff calls the Christian evaluation that recognizes both the positive and negative side of human responses to God "an example of pure dialectic: two contrasting assessments that are inseparably linked, . . . they do not cancel each other out, nor do they fuse in Hegelian fashion into a higher synthesis."[2] This dialectical position is just as insistent as Barth's on the distinction between revelation and religion and on the human creativity involved in religion. It attempts to follow the biblical witness in its assessment of religion, and since it sees the biblical view of human religion as more negative than positive, it tends to emphasize the negative evaluation of religion.

For all three kinds of neo-Reformation interpretation, the completely or partially or dialectically negative view of religion is important for Christian theology. Christian faith should recognize that it is not religion, and Christian theology should build, not on the universal human capacity to be religious, but on the particular revelation of God in a particular history.

The one neo-Reformation theologian who tried to give equal hand to the Catholic emphasis on the positive value of human religion and to the Protestant critique of religion was Gerardus van der Leeuw, who therefore had the most two-sided approach to the Christian theologians' utilization of the concept of religion. On the one hand, all of Christian life can be viewed as part and parcel of the total human religious effort. But on the other hand, Christian life can also be viewed, not as human effort and human construction, but as God's gift in Christ. Christian theologians, insists van der Leeuw, must try alternately to look at Christian life in both these ways.

W.C. SMITH'S CHALLENGE
TO THE CONCEPT OF RELIGION

Van der Leeuw is known to the scholarly world outside of his own country, the Netherlands, not as a theologian but as a historian of religion. Still another and quite different kind of challenge to the Christian theologians' concept of religion has also been developed by a historian of religion, Professor Wilfred Cantwell Smith. In his book *The Meaning and End of Religion*, published in 1963, Dr. Smith shocked some of his colleagues and intrigued all of his readers by arguing that

neither religion in general nor any one of the religions . . . is in itself an intelligible entity, a valid object of inquiry or of concern either for the scholar or for the man of faith. Men throughout history and throughout the world have been able to *be* religious without the assistance of a special term, without the intellectual analysis that the term implies. . . . In some ways it is probably easier to be religious without the concept . . . . The notion of religion can become an enemy of piety. One might almost say that the concern of the religious man is with God; the concern of the observer is with religion.[3]

Wilfred Cantwell Smith has a criticism of religion very different from that of Karl Barth. Barth assumes that religion is a certain kind of reality in human life and then subjects that human reality to a very complex and searching evaluation in the light of God's revelation apprehended in Christian faith. Wilfred Smith, on the other hand, questions whether "religion" is a reality at all and suggests that it is a relatively modern and western concept that distorts human religiousness more than it comprehends it. Professor Smith is addressing a somewhat different audience than Barth's, for Smith is speaking most directly to his own colleagues in the academic study of religion. It is possible that my initial negative reaction, and that of many of my colleagues, was influenced by some professional defensiveness. If we've come to the "end of religion," we professional students of religion might be out of business! It should be said that much of the positive response to Smith's book comes from his focusing much inchoate dissatisfaction within the academic establishment of the study of religion.

What of Christian theologians? Is this effort to challenge the reality of our modern western notion of religion of concern to them? Wilfred Smith certainly intended and intends to be saying something of relevance to Christian theologians and in his more recent thinking he has turned more and more directly to the task of theological interpretation. But quite apart from his own theological work, it should be obvious that his critique challenges much Christian interpretation of "other religions" in this century. Clearly the discussion must be put in different terms if the "other religions" are not *out there* in the reality of human life but are the product of our own faulty conception, a distortion produced by our own mental spectacles.

Wilfred Smith has certainly shown that "religion" is a western concept and has successfully challenged any naive realism that assumes that the cultural life of the rest of the world does in fact have just the shape in which it presents itself to our modern western minds. Some may be unhappy with an implicit nominalism in this kind of critique, the suggestion that all our concepts are *mere* concepts. He does in fact suggest alternative concepts to that of "religion." He argues that "cumulative tradition" and "faith" between them much more adequately grasp the reality of human religiousness than do the concretized abstractions we commonly call "religions."

Professor Smith has forced me to face the fact that "religion" is, at the least, a western concept, and he has given an illuminating sketch of the evolution of this concept. It is this very history, however, that has led me to much more positive conclusions about the utility of this concept for the Christian theologian reflecting on the multifaceted realm of human culture that we have called religion.

Both the general concept or concepts of "religion" and the whole glossary of "religious" concepts we have come to employ have developed in three streams from medieval western Christian language: (1) Roman Catholic theology and practice since the sixteenth century, (2) Protestant theology and practice, and (3) Enlightenment rationalism. The medieval Christian conceptual language existed both in West European vernaculars and in Latin. The Latin terminology was itself an earlier "translation language," which made use of the available concepts in Roman and late Hellenistic culture to translate the Christian Scriptures from Hebrew and Greek and to express Christian piety. The result of this process of translation was a whole new vocabulary that pointed religiously in two directions: (1) to earlier linguistic and cultural matrices of Christianity in Palestine, Syria, Egypt, and Asia Minor and (2) to classical Roman culture and later Hellenistic-Roman culture. A vocabulary was created in which every term pointed to both similarity and difference between the new Christian piety and the pre-Christian culture. There was similarity, because the same term could be employed, and there was difference, because the new piety was very different, both in general and in particulars, and often called for a painful break with the pre-Christian culture. In certain terms, the novelty was more important than the continuity, and in others, the continuing meaning was more significant than the novelty. It is crucial to our present discussion that *fides* ("faith") and *credo* ("I believe") are examples of the first development; they acquired an almost totally new content in their Christian usage. *Religio, pietas,* and *devotio,* on the other hand, are terms that retained much of their pre-Christian meaning.

The Roman concept of *religio* was already complex. Its two presumed etymologies each pointed to a different dimension. One focused on ritual practice. We can trace its development from its pre-Christian definition by Lucretius to its post-Christian usage by the Bible translator Jerome and much of both medieval and modern Roman Catholic practice. The other dimension was that of inner piety. It is emphasized in Cicero's pre-Christian definition as well as in Augustine's Christian theology, and it is the dimension carried forward by the Protestant reformer Zwingli and the post-Enlightenment Protestant theologian Schleiermacher.

The first extensive use of this western concept of religion outside of Western Europe was by the Jesuit missionaries in the sixteenth, seventeenth, and eighteenth centuries. Their reports on "religion" in many parts of the world were turned to a use very different from the Jesuit missionaries' intentions by the Enlightenment rationalists of the eighteenth-century and their successors, both rationalist and romantic, in the nineteenth and twentieth centuries. "Natural religion," whether positively or negatively evaluated, was independent of Christian thought and Christian religious practice.

The concept of religion goes back to western Christian translation language, and that, in turn, goes back to the Christian willingness to *translate* their sacred Scriptures into other languages, perhaps derived from the Hellenistic Jews' decision to translate the Hebrew Bible into Greek. The willingness to translate sacred words presupposes a confidence in a common element in human language and thus in human nature. A common element makes it possible for sacred truths to be expressed in another language. We are now so familiar with the process of translation as Christians that we may not understand how daring an undertaking was the Hellenistic Jews' translation of the Hebrew Bible, nor how important was their belief in the divine guidance of that translation. If we survey human religious practice, however, we see that translation or retranslation of sacred scriptures and liturgies has often been forbidden and very often, including in Christian circles, been viewed with deep suspicion.

I suggest that the human universal "religion" is by a circuitous route derived from early and later Christian confidence in the universal comprehensibility of the Christian message and the universal applicability of Christian piety. The divine Word can be expressed in differing human words because that divine Word is somehow behind every human being capable of uttering words.

The development of the western concept of religion has been like a snowball rolling downhill. It has worked on the principle of analogy: Something out there is somewhat like something we already call religious, and that new something, for example, the Melanesian notion of *tabu*, sticks to the concept and permanently enlarges it. Sometimes, of course, such a snowball hits a bush or a tree trunk, which may break off part of the accretion on one side, or even split the snowball altogether. Perhaps Smith's *The Meaning and End of Religion* is such a tree trunk! In any case, the part of the process of development of which Professor Smith most disapproves is the reification, the hardening into supposedly independent and real things, of the various "religions." The more Christianity was conceived as a self-contained intellectual system, the more other forms of human piety were thought of analogously as separate cultural systems called "religions." What Professor Smith has suggested is not really to stop this thinking by analogy, but to refine it. He is saying more than that the notion of a "religion" is typically western. He is saying that if religious life in China is misconceived by construing it as the interpenetration of three or four "religions," and if Hindu piety is misconceived by calling it Hinduism, then Christian religious life might also be misunderstood by thinking of it as "the Christian religion," regardless of how familiar that abstraction has become since the Enlightenment.

In any case, I think it is possible to refine the concept of religion by becoming conscious of false analogies and being more discriminating in applying familiar terms to strange phenomena. Even if we were to reject the word "religion," however, we should either have to abandon efforts at intercultural understanding or find some new term that would point to areas of human thought and feeling and activity that we have been accustomed to designate with the western term "religion." We could seek some term from another religious context, such as the Sanskrit term *dharma* or the Arabic term *dīn,* and see whether such a term could be expanded to do general service. Or we could seek some neutral term that would apply equally well in all cultures. Or we could take some other western religious term and seek to generalize upon it. Perhaps "cumulative tradition" is an example of a neutral "scientific term," and "faith" seems to be an example of another western religious term. I believe that "faith" is a Christian term that has close Jewish and Islamic parallels. Elsewhere the equivalents are harder to find, for faith is more closely bound than religion to characteristically Christian religiousness and does not have such a firm root as "religion" in the pre-Christian world of antiquity.

The particular word we choose to use as the most general concept is of less concern to Christian theologians than the presence in their thinking of a concept that links them as directly and deeply as possible to all of humanity outside the Christian community, for Christian faith is not true to its own heritage if it is expressed in terms only intelligible to Christian believers. It is in our common humanity that God speaks a creative and redeeming word to us and it is as members of the human race that we are enjoined to convey God's love.

It is the confidence in our common humanity that underlies the *concept* of religion. Whether the concept is useful depends on whether it can point to a common human *reality*. I believe that in an atmosphere of critical western self-consciousness and intercultural dialogue it can perform that service and that indeed because of its peculiar western history it can contribute to a more than western and more than simply Christian goal of interreligious understanding. Some theologians of the ancient Christian church saw manifold evidence of the divine Logos in the noblest of pre-Christian philosophies. It should not be forgotten that some of the same theologians were more negative about what we think of as "religion," the cults of the Hellenistic world, seeing them as Satanic imitations of the true cult of Christ. They would have found very strange the modern notion that both philosophical speculation and religious ritual are the product of merely human inventiveness. We may yet find some synthesis of our modern sophistication and the wisdom of the ancient church. Religion is an aspect of our common humanity and an area of our human creativity, but it can be both superhuman and subhuman. God fights against the demonic powers in the heights and depths of the human religious consciousness, not as puppeteer pulling strings, but as one who has joined us in the struggle and wrested victory from defeat.

SOME LIMITS TO THE THEOLOGICAL UTILITY OF RELIGION

The concept of religion continues to be meaningful to Christian theologians, and the mysterious area of human life to which it points is an area of real, if paradoxical, value. Nevertheless, there are limits to the theological utility of this concept. One hint of such limits is the fact that religion is not a biblical concept. It shares that distinction with much of our traditional theological vocabulary, but at least for a Protestant theologian the nonbiblical concept in theology should flash a yellow warning light: proceed with caution.

Religion is a useful concept for relating Christian existence to many common dimensions of human culture. Both our common aspirations toward transcendence and our common sinfulness are widely and diversely exemplified in the world of human religion. But the concepts pointing toward common elements of human life are necessarily abstract and tend to subordinate the specific instance to the general category. Where we are concerned with a particular community with its own particular history, the abstract concepts of religion may be less helpful. This may be especially true when we are looking at our own religious history and the relation of our own religious communities to those related to us by common or intersecting histories. The problem is most acute when a community believes itself called out of the common life of humanity, the life of the Nations or Gentiles, to the special burdens of being chosen as a special people.

While the concepts of religion may be helpful in Jewish-Christian dialogue, and while human religiousness can surely be richly exemplified from Jewish experience, there may be more biblical concepts than religion that should be central in Christian efforts to understand Jewish existence. It is possible that, with some revisions, the concepts of "religion" might be more appropriate to Jewish efforts to understand Christian existence, since for Jews Christians are among the descendants of Noah, subject to the requirements of God's general covenant with humankind, but not party to God's covenant with Abraham, let alone heir to the divine law given through Moses.

The general concepts of religion are also not the most helpful ones in Christian-Muslim dialogue, in which the Christian situation with relation to the Jews is reversed. It is the Muslims who have a comprehensive *Heilsgeschichte* that provides a basis for their relation with Jews and Christians, and it is the Christians who generally do not recognize the Book or the Prophet or the People of God in the Muslim witness.

OUR PRESENT CONTEXT
FOR THEOLOGICAL REFLECTION AND DIALOGUE

Some may be wondering whether this very academic discussion has any relevance for that conversation in the Ramayapatnam clinic. It has relevance, but it is indirect. For if I returned to Ramayapatnam tomorrow, I should still be unable to communicate in the appropriate local idiom. It's even clearer to me now than it was then that there is an important distinction between telling the story of God's love in Jesus Christ, reflecting on the implications of that story with other Christians, and trying to understand and be understood in a situation of inter-religious dialogue. Those distinctions are clear enough in theory, but the way we actually meet people is often like the encounter in the clinic. We should not despise the requirements of academic clarity, but in a particular situation of meeting with other people we need to have a concrete word, especially a gospel word of encouragement, but sometimes also a prophetic word of admonition or warning. If I were to return to my *classroom* in Ramayapatnam, I would hope that I should at least be able to help Telugu theological students, who stand much closer to the particular needs of local villagers than I ever could. I would hope that they could communicate to those to whom they preach and whom they counsel that they share with them much of the traditional world of religion as well as the modern world of rapid social change, and that the healing and enlightenment of Christ are appropriate to both traditional and modern contexts.

A more important question, however, concerns our current situation in the West, for it is here that most of us are at work. What is the appropriate setting here to consider "the Christian church in a religiously plural world?" What is the religious situation in which such thinking must take place, and what notion of religion, if any, is relevant to that theological reflection? This entire conference at Washington and Lee is tackling those questions. I want to point out how significant it is that this discussion will take place, not in a theological seminary, but under the auspices of a college department of religion. Many seminaries in the United States are so parochial in their concerns that the problem before this conference is simply not a live issue. There are other, much more liberal theological schools, on the other hand, that have such a broad view of theology or religious studies that the question before this conference seems itself too parochial, and, in any case, no more a live issue than for more conservative schools. Where Christian theology is completely identified with the general study of religion, the question before this conference simply disappears for the theologian. But since the question continues to be a real problem for the Christian community in many parts of the world, including many parts of this country, such theology fails to provide the intellectual guidance that the church needs.

It might seem that a college religion department would be the last place to locate a Christian theological discussion. There are indeed departments that would be extremely uncomfortable with the word "theology," let alone with an issue of practical relevance for a particular religious community. There are other religion departments, however, in which recent efforts to redress past Protestant Christian dominance have led to a new situation, not of theological indifference, but of more self-conscious religious pluralism, and in some places, also to a genuine inter-religious exchange.

The most significant development is the growth of such exchange between Jews and Christians, but it is ironic that the platform for such discussion should be furnished by the concept of religion, a tool originally fashioned by Christians to comprehend their relation to other Gentiles.

Both Christians and Muslims claim that they share with Jews the faith of Abraham. Christians should recognize how strange that claim must sound to Jews, much stranger than the Arab claim to kinship through Ishmael, for the Christians' claim to be "children of the promise" rests upon their miraculous kinship with Jesus and the community of Jesus' disciples. Yet however strange the claim, Christian theologians should not abandon it, for it is the faith of Abraham that gives much of the distinctive shape to Christian existence. This special claim should not be confused with the kinship of Christians, in their creation, their fall, and their redemption, with all of humanity.

Abraham's faith is neither the essence of religion nor the opposite of religion; it is one particular and distinctive form of human religion.

Christians need to face alternately in what at first seem to be opposite directions. We need to recognize that we are part of the Gentiles, i.e., the "Nations" who stand outside and over against the people of Israel. On the other hand, we believe that we have been miraculously added to the people of Israel, not instead of but in addition to those who can claim physical descent from the patriarchs and the sons of Jacob. Thus we face toward the Gentiles in our sharing of religion, and we face toward Israel in our sharing of the covenants. That difference in stance is not an absolute distinction, however, for what joins all humanity is not so much our common descent from the primordial pair as our sharing in the divine rescue of Noah and his family, in the universal promise attested by the rainbow, and in the common human obligations of mortality.

Christian theologians should no longer be blind to our *religious* kinship with all other human beings; but where we are joined by a history within that common humanity, it is an evasion of truth not to recognize that fact, however complex or painful that history may be. The story of Noah suggests, however, that behind the discernible history is a broader history that encompasses *all* creatures, not only human creatures, in the rescue of God and the promise of God. The theologian has a double task: to find in our common humanity the basis of an ever new translation of the good news of God, and to trace the history of God's choice of a special people sustained in order to work for the healing of all nations. Encompassing that double task is the ancient story of the rainbow covenant and the future vision of the peaceable kingdom.

NOTES

1. Karl Rahner, *The Church: Readings in Theology,* compiled at the Canisianum, Innsbruck (New York: P.J. Kenedy and Sons, 1953), pp. 118–19.

2. F.W.A. Korff, *Het Christelijk Geloof en de Niet-Christelijke Godsdiensten* (Amsterdam: Holland Uitgeversmaatschappij, 1946), pp. 79–83, 100.

3. Wilfred Cantwell Smith, *The Meaning and End of Religion* (New York: Macmillan, 1963), pp. 12,19.

7

Religion as a Problem
for the Christian Mission

Gerald H. Anderson

Dr. Carman begins his essay with an autobiographical confession—an experience he had as a graduate student in India—which leads him to a discussion of our theme. I want to do the same.

Twenty years ago when Hendrik Kraemer's book *Religion and the Christian Faith* was published, I was a graduate student at the Ecumenical Institute near Geneva, Switzerland, where Dr. Kraemer had earlier been the director. In a seminar discussion of the book that winter there were, among others, a German theological student, a Methodist pastor from Ceylon, and myself. Several things stick vividly in my memory from that seminar, because—in a very real sense—it changed the course of my life.

First, the German student. He had studied at Basel and had acquired the uncanny capacity to quote something from Karl Barth on virtually every issue that came up in any discussion, and he never could understand why some of us were not completely dazzled by Barth's view of all religion apart from the biblical revelation as simply "unbelief."[1] Midway through our study of Kraemer's book we all made a pilgrimage to Basel and spent a few hours with Dr. Barth. Each of us had the opportunity to ask him a question, and my question was whether he could say *anything* positive about the revealing and redeeming activity of God within the non-Christian religions as such. His answer, in substance, was "No."[2]

The second thing I remember about the seminar was my utter disappointment and dissatisfaction with Kraemer's failure to move beyond the narrow views he had expressed in his 1938 book, *The Christian Message in a Non-Christian World.*[3] In the earlier book he said that Christianity was "*the* religion of revelation" (p. 23), and he stressed a radical discontinuity between the realm of what he called "biblical realism" (which critics said was neither biblical nor realistic) and the whole range of non-Christian religious experience.[4] Now in the later book Kraemer granted that God is somehow active in the non-Christian religions through various "modes of revelation" (nature, history, and conscience), but he concluded that these are in the final analysis "figments of thought at times useful as instruments but they do not represent anything real" (pp. 354–57).[5] I was not persuaded by this exclusivistic type of Christocentrism, and my objections to it in the seminar led to the third experience which I recall.

The Methodist pastor from Ceylon in our seminar was an ardent devotee of Kraemer's Barthian views, and was troubled that I—a fellow Methodist—was so unappreciative of them. One day in the midst of our seminar, he turned to me and said, "I hope you never come to Asia as a missionary because with your theology you will do more harm than good." I took that very seriously and prayed about it a great deal over the next several months. I concluded that if my theology—in particular my theology of mission in terms of the Christian attitude and approach to persons of other faiths—was fundamentally inadequate to work in Asia, then it was also inadequate to work in North America or anywhere else.

Therefore when I returned to Boston University to complete my graduate studies I decided to write my doctoral dissertation on the theology of mission as it has developed among Protestants in the twentieth century. After I wrote the dissertation, I went to Southeast Asia as a missionary for ten years. As a footnote to this story I should report that twelve years after the seminar in Switzerland I visited Ceylon, and my Methodist pastor friend there invited me to preach in his church. When I reminded him about what he had said concerning my theology and the harm that I might do, he laughed and said that he had already taken it into consideration and had decided that he would be able to repair whatever damage I might do with just one sermon.

My experience in that seminar and my subsequent theological pilgrimage—in reaction to Kraemer's dead-end concept of "radical discontinuity," which dominated nearly a generation of Protestant missionary thinking—is not untypical of the shift in attitudes in North America and certain other parts of the world, notably in Asia.[6] We look back now and see that—as M.M. Thomas has observed—Kraemer turned on a red light in 1938, stopping the Christian traffic with other religions, and never changed it to green, so that a whole generation of Protestants, for the most part, stood still, "isolated from the dynamic movements in other religions and the adherents of the renascent faiths."[7] All of that has changed now, of course, and we are in quite a different era of attitudes and approaches on the part of Protestants toward persons of other faiths, and—as Dr. Carman has indicated—the shift is even more pronounced among Roman Catholics.

Part of the problem for the Christian theologian in dealing with the theme of this symposium is that there are *two* distinct traditions in the history of Christian thought, both unsupported by the witness of the New Testament, concerning the relationship between Christianity and other religious traditions, between Christian faith and other faiths.[8]

One of these is what we have already described as *discontinuity*. In this tradition the non-Christian religions are viewed as the various efforts of human beings to apprehend their existence, whereas Christianity is the result of the self-disclosure of God in Jesus Christ. God has spoken to humanity only in the person of Jesus Christ, and "there is salvation in no one else" (Acts 4:12).

The other tradition, while recognizing the uniqueness and universality of Jesus Christ, emphasizes the *continuity* of God's revealing and redeeming activity in Christ with his activity among all persons everywhere. It views Christian faith as the climax of a divine revelation that began long before human history and has been available to everyone. Jesus Christ, in this view, is crucial, normative, and definitive, but not exclusive. What is true of Jesus Christ in a focal way is pervasively true of the whole cosmos. He is the key or clue to the rest of God's working. But the Word of God is not limited to the revelation in the historic person of Jesus. There is much biblical and patristic testimony in support of this tradition also. John's Gospel affirms that the same light which was in Jesus enlightens everyone (John 1:1–9). Paul said that a thousand years before the birth of Jesus, "Christ" was with the Israelites in their wanderings in Sinai (1 Cor. 10:4). And Acts 14:17 assures us that "God did not leave himself without witness" even among those who knew nothing of the biblical revelation. In this view, the *logos spermatikos* is active everywhere, sowing seeds of truth, and thus preparing the way for the gospel. Justin Martyr went so far as to say that before Jesus was born "those who lived according to reason are Christians, even though they have been thought atheists; as among the Greeks, Socrates and Heraclitus and men like them" (*I Apology*, 46). Recent contributions to this tradition include Paul Tillich's concept of "the latent church" and Karl Rahner's thought about "the anonymous presence of God" in the non-Christian world.

The history of Christian thinking on the theme of this conference has been very largely a shifting of emphasis between one or the other of these two traditions and their many variations. There is broad consensus now, however, that further debate in terms of continuity and discontinuity would be fruitless, largely because it is meaningful only to those who share the Greco-Roman mentality—that is, in the old centers of theological influence in Europe and North America, and in the remaining outposts of triumphal Teutonic theological tribalism in the so-called Third World.

New conceptual terms and categories are required to break through the stalemate, and these are most likely to come from the new centers of theological vitality in Asia, Africa, and Latin America—where the majority of Christians will be living in the year 2000.[9] We of the West, as Max Warren has urged, should trust the Holy Spirit to lead the Christians of the Third World as they seek to reconceptualize the God of biblical revelation within the context of their different cultures.

What new initiatives have emerged in the post-Kraemer period toward understanding the "Christian faith in a religiously plural world" in categories other than continuity/ discontinuity? The question is worthy of several doctoral dissertations (some have already been written[10]), and we can mention only a few instances that illustrate the situation. As recently as 1968, Willem A. Bijlefeld wrote in his article "Trends in the Contemporary Discussion on 'Christians and Men of Other Faiths' " that

> the crucial point for Protestants and Roman Catholics alike is indeed this one: do we dare to face and discuss honestly and openly the question whether there is still any place for the church as a particular social entity and a separate religious community in an environment conditioned and to a large extent determined by another culture and religious tradition than Christianity? . . . As long as we stress the need of a transformation from within one religious community into another, we are still dealing with "continuity or discontinuity." . . . The plea for proclaiming the Gospel not only initially, but as a permanent structure "within Hindu (Muslim, Buddhist) culture and religion" is the only real move beyond Tambaram 1938 of which I know.[11]

Since 1968 a good deal of momentum has developed. This has been generated largely through the efforts of the Vatican Secretariat for Non-Christian Religions, and through the programs of the World Council of Churches on "Dialogue with People of Living Faiths and Ideologies." Especially important are the twenty-one centers for study and dialogue with persons of other faiths in Asia, Africa, Latin America, and the Middle East that are affiliated with the World Council of Churches.[12]

These centers have a fourfold emphasis:[13]

—to help the churches to deepen their commitment to Jesus Christ and to rediscover the content and practice of mission in situations of cultural and religious pluralism;

—to provide them with guidelines for their actual engagement with people of different faiths and ideologies with whom they are in daily contact and through whose cooperation the work of social renewal and nation-building must go on;

—to examine the relationship between the Christian faith and other faiths, not just on the conceptual level but in the context of Christian communities living in dialogue and shared humanity with their neighbors of other faiths; and

—to see how the church's confession of Jesus Christ as Lord and Savior and as the initiator of a new humanity may, at the same time, be related to the common humanity which we all share with people of other faiths and ideologies.

M. M. Thomas, sometime director of the Christian Institute for the Study of Religion and Society in Bangalore, India, proposes that "today we are engaged in discovering a post-liberal and post-Kraemer theology of religion which emphasizes a common humanity in Christ rather than a common religiosity. We have not yet come to anything like an adequate understanding of what God has been and is doing in and with other religions."[14]

On the question of the relation of dialogue to evangelism, the Bangkok 1973 conference on "Salvation Today" (which invited a group of Buddhists in Thailand to present *their* understanding of salvation to the conference) said, "A desire to share and a readiness to let others share with us should inspire our witness to Christ rather than a desire to win a theological argument."[15]

The plea of W. Cantwell Smith through the 1960s was—and still is—for the church to "work vigorously, and work on a large scale, in order to construct an adequate doctrine" that will avoid "the fallacy of relentless exclusivism" and affirm "the kind of God whom Jesus Christ has revealed Him to be"—namely, the God who "reaches out after all men everywhere, and speaks to all who will listen."[16] Smith's particular proposals for shifting the discussion in Christian thought concerning "religion" and "religions" to new ground came in his books *The Meaning and End of Religion* and *Questions of Religious Truth,* to which Dr. Carman addresses himself.

I have several problems with Dr. Smith's proposals. First, I

am uncomfortable with discussing religions in terms of truth
and falsity and I do not think it is necessary to employ these
categories—at least with the insistence that Dr. Smith has
applied them in his *Questions of Religious Truth*—in order to
speak of religions as such. As a missionary, as a seminary
professor, and as a pastor, I don't think I have ever claimed
that Christianity is true. I do affirm what Jesus said of Himself:
"I am the way, and the truth, and the life; no one comes to the
Father, but by me" (John 14:6). In his *Questions of Religious
Truth* Smith asks, "But what would you mean by saying that it
[the religious life of a given tribe] is true or false?" The answer
is that I wouldn't say it; that is not my prerogative. Rather, I
would affirm with D. T. Niles that "it is outside the preacher's
competence or commission to pass judgment on what others
claim to be their experience of salvation; his business is only to
invite them to acknowledge Jesus Christ as their Savior."[17]

Second, while I am persuaded by Dr. Smith that our contemporary concept of religion(s) is a relatively modern and
western systematizing process, I am not convinced that this
therefore makes the concept unfeasible, or that his "alternate
theoretical framework for interpreting to ourselves the religious history of man" has fewer problems. What I do realize is
that we western Christians must be increasingly open to Third
World refinements, revisions, and reconceptualizing of our
western concepts—and that, after all, is the main thrust of Dr.
Smith's concern. As John Carman rightly points out:

The particular word we choose to use as the most general concept is of
less concern to Christian theologians than the presence in their thinking of a concept that links them as directly and deeply as possible to all
of humanity outside the Christian community. . . . It is the confidence in our common humanity that underlies the *concept* of religion.
Whether the concept is useful depends on whether it can point to a
common human *reality*.

Third, I am troubled by Dr. Smith's emphasis on a
personalized—almost privatized—conception of revelation
and religious truth. "Christianity," he says, "is not true absolutely, impersonally, statically; rather, it can *become* true, if and

as you or I appropriate it to ourselves and interiorize it, insofar as we live it out from day to day. It becomes true as we take it off the shelf and personalize it."[18] This is an important corrective against embalmed faith. On the other hand, Christ does not *become* the truth when or because we experience him as such. The kingdom of God is not a democracy and Jesus Christ—as Lord and Savior—is not going out of office if we do not vote for him.[19]

Let me also mention the prognosis of Professor John Hick at the University of Birmingham, England, on the future course of the world religions, because he represents another variation—albeit an extreme one—in the Christian tradition of continuity. He anticipates that somewhere in the future

what we now call different religions will constitute the past history of different emphases and variations within something that it need not be too misleading to call a single world religion. . . . I mean that the discoveries now taking place by men of different faiths of central common ground . . . may eventually render obsolete the sense of belonging to rival ideological communities. . . . Thus we may expect the different world faiths to continue as religious-cultural phenomena, though phenomena that are increasingly interpenetrating one another. The relation between them will then be somewhat like that now obtaining between the different denominations of Christianity.[20]

That, I submit, is more the vision of a philosopher than of a Christian theologian. There is virtually nothing in the New Testament or in the experience of the church to support such a vision. In this view the church is hardly the church and—understandably—Jesus Christ is not mentioned. Whenever the church falls into *sub*-mission, failing faithfully to witness to the unique, ultimate, and universal lordship of Jesus Christ over all of God's creation, it soon ceases to be the church.

By contrast, the forecast from Dr. Dawe in our conference is that "all claims to universality have to be related to the fact that no particular religion will be the sole religion of humankind." I take it that he does not anticipate a convergence of the world religions—à la John Hick—but rather is reminding us of the thoroughly biblical perspective that the church is called, not to be successful, but to be faithful. Two things, however, need to be emphasized. First, this does not relieve the church of the biblical mandate for "the evangelization of the world," unless—as Bishop Stephen Neill has warned—one is prepared to rewrite the New Testament and take it out. Second, the New Testament also affirms the ultimate triumph or consummation of God's righteousness and sovereign purpose for his whole creation in the eschatological kingdom revealed in Jesus Christ, of which Professor Dawe speaks.

In closing, let me draw attention to a Christian voice from Asia that we in the West need to hear as we reflect on the way God relates to creation and the ways in which various peoples respond to God. Dr. Choan-Seng Song, formerly professor of theology at Tainan Theological College in Taiwan and now associate director of the Faith and Order Commission in the World Council of Churches, complains that western Christian theologians "obstinately persist in reflecting on Asian or African cultures and histories from the vantage-point of that messianic hope which is believed to be lodged in the history of the Christian Church, . . . and redemption loses its intrinsic meaning for cultures and histories outside the history of Christianity." Song believes this is "a distortion of the message of the Bible," and he is "convinced that a very big theological blunder has been committed by those theologians who have forced God's redemption into the history of a nation [Israel] and of the Christian Church, and have consequently institutionalized it." Contrary to the traditional western understanding of "salvation history," Song argues that the Old Testament "prophetic tradition consists in a refusal to recognize the history of Israel as identifiable with the totality of God's acts in the redemption of his creation." Israel was *not* to be "the nation through which God's redeeming love would be mediated, *but* to be a symbol of how God would also deal redemptively with other nations." Therefore, says Song, other nations can learn from the experience of Israel "how their histories can be interpreted redemptively. . . . An Asian nation will thus be enabled to find its place side by side with

Israel in God's salvation." This "theological leap" from the experience of Israel to the cultures and histories of other peoples and nations is consistent, according to Song, with the radical interruption in history of "the Word become flesh" and with "the dialectic of salvation revealed to us through the witness in the Bible."[21]

In this way, he says,

The history of salvation to which the Bible gives witness is not a closed history. It is an open-ended history always seeking the application of its proto-model beyond itself. We may call this the task of the proto-model in search of sub-models in cultures outside the Judeo-Christian tradition. The proto-model in the primary culture and history of the Judeo-Christian world finds fulfillment in its sub-models in the secondary cultures and histories outside the Judeo-Christian world. The task of Christian theology in Asia consists, among other things, in perceptive and systematic interpretation of sub-models brought out from hiddenness into visibility as the result of the application of the proto-model.[22]

Song's "theological leap" should force some western theologians to rethink their traditional understanding of the way God deals with "the Nations." But his leap may also have taken him too far toward the democratization of *heilsgeschichte*, if the sub-models (to use his terms) are only to be "brought out from hiddenness into visibility" and interpreted, but not judged and transformed, "as the result of the application of the proto-model." The goal of the gospel is to bring about change or transformation into something new, which will correspond with what has been revealed in the life and teaching of Jesus Christ. That is always the problem for Christian theology as it faces religion—including its own.

NOTES

1. D. T. Niles recalled that in his first meeting with Karl Barth in 1935, Barth said, "Other religions are just unbelief." Niles asked, "How many Hindus, Dr. Barth, have you met?" Barth answered, "No one." Niles said, "How then do you know that Hinduism is unbelief?" Barth replied, "A priori." Niles concluded, "I simply shook my head and smiled" (D. T. Niles, "Karl Barth—A Personal Memory," *The South East Asia Journal of Theology* 11 [Autumn 1969]: 10–11).

2. Barth had written earlier that "the discussion as to whether there is not revelation also in other religions is superfluous. . . . 'Revelations' which are different from that which has taken place and which is still taking place in Him, we can only call 'revelations' in a perverted, invalid, and loose sense of the concept" (*Revelation*, ed. John Baillie and Hugh Martin [New York: Macmillan, 1937], p. 45).

3. Kraemer said that the new book was "without any real change in my standpoints of 1938" (pp. 232–33).

4. L. Harold DeWolf raised the fundamental question about Kraemer's position: "All the religions, including Christianity, he says, are relative; only the Christian revelation is absolute. Yet he assumes that he knows this revelation. But does not his interpretation of the revelation and its requirement of us constitute a part of religion, if not the religion of the Church, then at least the religion of Hendrik Kraemer? On what ground does Kraemer's understanding of the Word escape the relativism of all religion? If his understanding of the Word is, even in some respects, human and relative, then why should we accept this part of it, namely the doctrine of *discontinuity*, without the proofs required of any other human idea which claims identity with divine truth?" (*The Theology of the Christian Mission*, ed. Gerald H. Anderson [New York: McGraw-Hill, 1961], p. 208).

5. Much has been made of the fact that Barth and Kraemer viewed Christianity along with all other religion and religions as under the judgment of the Word of God revealed in Jesus Christ. At the same time, however, they allowed that "the Church by grace lives through grace, and to this extent is the embodiment of the true religion," and that "as an act of faith" it is possible to speak of Christianity as "the true religion" (Kraemer discussing Barth's position, *Religion and the Christian Faith*, pp. 188–89). Kraemer had described Christianity in his earlier book as "*the* religion of revelation" (p. 23), and said that "empirical Christianity has stood and stands under continuous and direct influence and judgment of the revelation in Christ and is in virtue thereof in a different position from the other religions" (p. 145). In both books Kraemer said he was addressing the question: "From the standpoint of the Christian Revelation . . . does God—and if so, how and where does God—reveal Himself in the religious life as present in the *non-Christian religions?*" (*Religion and the Christian Faith*, p. 233, emphasis added).

6. Just a few weeks after giving this paper at the Washington and Lee University symposium, Dr. Carman and I participated in a consultation on "Asian and African Contributions to Contemporary Theology" at the Ecumen-

ical Institute in Switzerland, where another Methodist pastor from Ceylon (now Sri Lanka) read a paper, "Towards a Theology of Dialogue." In it he said, "The Christian faith has its distinctive character in that it is about Jesus Christ and that it announces the in-breaking of the rule of God over all life, but this gives no additional validity to what can be historically traced as the Christian religion. . . . There can be nothing sacrosanct, therefore, about its form, mode or life." He emphasized that "the whole concept of 'salvation history,' understood as the history of the Jewish nation and the Church, is to be seriously challenged by the theologians of Asia and Africa. . . . One must affirm that salvation history is the history of the whole of humankind. Dialogue cannot take place in a true spirit of discernment if the parties involved exclude each other's history from the mainstream of the salvation that God offers to all people" (S. Wesley Ariarajah, "Towards a Theology of Dialogue," *The Ecumenical Review* [Geneva] 29, no. 1 [January 1977]: 5,11). It was especially interesting for me, not only that his statement documented my perception of the theological shift about which I had spoken at Washington and Lee, but that it was spoken virtually in the same room where I had been so vigorously challenged on these same points twenty years earlier, by another Methodist from Sri Lanka.

7. M. M. Thomas, "A Seminar on Kraemer," *Religion and Society* 5, no. 2 (June 1958): 63. Notto R. Thelle writes, "The captivating influence of Barthianism in Japan seemed to isolate Christian theology for many years and prevent it from engaging in a living dialogue with its spiritual environment" ("A Barthian Thinker Between Buddhism and Christianity. Takizawa Katsumi," *Japanese Religions* 8, no. 4 [October 1975]: 54). It has also been observed that "Barthian theology and nationalism flourished together in Japan and, interestingly, there was no resistance movement among Christians who held this theological position during the war" (Yoshinobu Kumazawa, "Japan: Where Theology Seeks to Integrate Text and Context," *Asian Voices in Christian Theology*, ed. Gerald H. Anderson [Maryknoll, N.Y.: Orbis Books, 1976], p. 189).

8. I have previously described these two traditions in my article on "Continuity and Discontinuity," in the *Concise Dictionary of the Christian World Mission*, ed. Stephen Neill, Gerald H. Anderson, and John Goodwin (Nashville: Abingdon Press, 1971), pp. 146–77.

9. This is the thesis we have advocated in *Asian Voices in Christian Theology*, and also in *Mission Trends No. 3* on the theme "Third World Theologies," ed. Gerald H. Anderson and Thomas F. Stransky (New York: Paulist Press and Grand Rapids: Eerdmans, 1976).

10. Most notably: Gérard Vallée, "From Tambaram to Uppsala, 1938–1968—An Ecumenical Debate on the Inter-religious Encounter," University of Münster, 1969; and Robert D. Young, *Encounter With World Religions* (Philadelphia: Westminster Press, 1970; originally a Ph.D. dissertation at Temple University, Philadelphia, Pa.). See also Carl F. Hallencrentz, *New Approaches to Men of Other Faiths, 1938–1968: A Theological Discussion* (Geneva: WCC, 1970); and Stanley J. Samartha, *Courage for Dialogue* (Maryknoll, N.Y.: Orbis Books, forthcoming).

11. *The Hartford Quarterly* 8, no. 3 (1968): 54–55. The plea to which Bijlefeld refers was that by Kaj Baago in "The Post-Colonial Crisis in Missions," *International Review of Mission* 55, no. 219 (July 1966): 322–32 and 56, no. 221 (January 1967): 99-103. See also the comments by Ian H. Douglas and John B. Carman on Baago's plea, *IRM* 55, no. 220 (October 1966): 483–89.

12. See S. J. Samartha, ed., *Dialogue Between Men of Living Faiths* (Geneva: WCC, 1971); Samartha, ed., *Living Faiths and Ultimate Goals: Salvation and World Religions* (Maryknoll, N.Y.: Orbis Books, 1975).

13. S. J. Samartha, "Christian Study Centres and Asian Churches," *International Review of Mission* 59, no. 234 (April 1970), 178–79.

14. *Religion and Society* 12, no. 3 (September 1965): 67.

15. David E. Johnson, ed., *Uppsala to Nairobi: 1968–1975* (New York: Friendship Press, 1975), p. 100.

16. Smith, "The Christian in a Religiously Plural World," *The Faith of Other Men* (New York: New American Library, 1963).

17. D. T. Niles, *The Preacher's Task and the Stone of Stumbling* (London: Lutterworth, 1958), pp. 32–33.

18. *Questions of Religious Truth* (New York: Harper & Row, 1972), p. 68.

19. See the critique of Smith by John Hick on this same point, in John Hick, ed., *Truth and Dialogue in World Religions: Conflicting Truth Claims* (Philadelphia: Westminster Press, 1974), pp. 143–49.

20. Ibid., pp. 151–52.

21. C. S. Song, "From Israel to Asia—A Theological Leap," *Mission Trends No. 3*, pp. 211 ff.

22. C. S. Song, "The Decisiveness of Christ," in *Asians and Blacks—Theological Challenges*, by C. S. Song and Gayraud Wilmore (Bangkok: East Asia Christian Conference, 1973), p. 25. Song also develops these points in his book, *Christian Mission in Reconstruction: An Asian Attempt* (Madras: Christian Literature Society, 1975; and Maryknoll, N.Y.: Orbis Books, 1977).

8

Religion and Revelation

Charles P. Price

I have been asked to respond to Professor Carman's searching and subtle paper in my capacity as a systematic theologian. You may remember the story of the day when God created the first theologian. He paused in dismay and called Satan to his side. "What have I done?" said the Lord. "I have made a creature so perfect in wisdom, power, and beauty that in the end he will rival even me." "Sire, it is easy," Satan replied. "Give him a colleague." We are all colleagues. What are we to make of religion in view of John Carman's proposals?

I should say at the outset that I conceive the task of Christian theology in a fairly conventional way, as reflection on Christian faith. Theology is *fides quaerens intellectum*, faith seeking understanding. The faith in question is faith in Jesus Christ recorded in the Scripture, mediated by the church. At least I mean it to be so. But the understanding involved is the understanding of a man who has to fix lawnmowers, make out income tax returns, contemplate computers and atoms, and live in a rapidly shrinking world. I also hold with certain philosophers that my work should "save the phenomena." Only a defective understanding of faith will describe an unrecognizable world.

Looming large among the phenomena with which one must reckon today are the great religious traditions of humankind. I would not always have said that. But I have been drawn more and more to recognize and ponder the importance of other faiths. The most vivid experience which has moved me in this direction came to me in connection with a seminar which I taught with Professor Carman at the Center for the Study of World Religions while I was still at Harvard. He asked me to give a course in basic Christianity at the Center for students of different faiths. What I learned was far more important than what I taught. For I met a group of men whose integrity, wisdom, commitment, and generosity of personal feeling I could only appreciate and admire. Despite our different backgrounds, we were one in our humanity. That experience is an important phenomenon which I believe to be crucial for a Christian theological system to preserve.

I

What struck me most forcibly about Professor Carman's paper was his insistence on the unity of humankind. "I suggest that the human universal 'religion,' " he told us, "is by a circuitous route derived from early and later Christian confidence in the universal comprehensibility of the Christian message and in the universal applicability of Christian piety. The divine Word can be expressed in differing words because that divine Word is somehow behind every human being capable of uttering words." Again, "The particular word we choose as the most general concept is of less concern to Christian theologians than the presence in their thinking of a concept that links them as directly and deeply as possible to all humanity." And at the end, "The theologian has a double task: to find in our common humanity the basis of an ever new translation of the good news of God and to trace the history of God's choice of a special people."

By mentioning the divine Word, Professor Carman in fact has let the cat out of the bag. The concept that seems to me to link us as directly and deeply as possible to all humankind is the divine Word, the Logos, which is the great theological expression of God's revelation of himself to us.

In the beginning was the Word, and the Word was with God, and the Word was God; all things were made through him, and without him was not anything made that was made. In him was life, and the life was the light of men. The light shines in the darkness, and the darkness has not overcome it. . . . The true light that enlightens every man was coming [or as the Greek text suggests *kept* coming] into the world (John 1:1ff.).

As Professor Carman's paper briefly indicated, eighteenth- and nineteenth-century thought about other religions picked up an older distinction between natural and revealed religion. The distinction had applied on the one hand to those elements of the Christian religion originally made known through the Scripture and to certain great dogmas, chiefly trinity and incarnation. All these were known by revelation. Christianity was revealed religion. Natural religion, on the other hand, applied to what could be known about God apart from revelation. As you know, the distinction was made at the beginning in order to accommodate Aristotelian philosophy to an existing body of Christian thought which had been elaborated in largely Platonic categories. The term "natural religion" was applied to non-Christian religions, as John Carman suggested, by Jesuit missionaries and Enlightenment philosophers. The reference was nothing short of disastrous for the conversation between Christianity and other religions. For it implied that the other religions of the world had nothing to do with the revelation of God. Revelation applied only to Christian religion.

Such a view involves an extraordinary idea of revelation, if one holds the radically monotheistic view of God which I believe the Bible teaches. I mean by "radical monotheism" the belief that there is but one God who is God of the whole cosmos. If anyone experiences God at all, it is this God who is experienced. There is no other. And my experience in teaching that seminar and other similar experiences have led me to affirm that there is true knowledge of God accessible in other religions. It comes from revelation. There is a category like it in most other religions, I think. And I do not believe that one comes to know ultimate reality by the exercise of finite human reason. I cannot know another person by the exercise of my own faculties unless the other chooses to reveal himself or herself to me. How much less could I know God apart from his self-revelation!

Consequently I have borrowed and perhaps misused a category from John Macquarrie. He speaks of *primordial revelation*. I should like to speak of primordial revelation in this sense: that human being emerges from the realm of all other beings when confronted with the holy and transcendent God in a new creative act. Human being is made possible when God reveals himself to the one made in his image.

Revelation continues. Human life is liberated, sustained, enhanced by the love of God, revealed to different peoples in different ways at critical times. It has not yet been said plainly enough at this conference, I think, that *revelation is salvation*. Revelation is distinguished from a warm fuzzy feeling by its saving quality. This is no private conclusion of my own, as I'm sure you know. I could find this idea expressed in Barth, Brunner, Tillich, and others. I regard it as a consensus of modern theology, at least modern Protestant theology. I do not know a great deal about world religions, but I'd expect to discover that in most if not all of them knowledge of God is connected with the yearly deliverance from the death of winter, or with a moment of illumination conceived as the liberation of life, or with a great historical rescue as at the Red Sea, or some similar moment. God reveals himself in many ways in many times beyond that primordial revelation of himself which makes us human.

All this is by way of appreciative elaboration of Professor Carman's desire to find some concept that links us directly and deeply with all humankind. I think that concept is revelation. I don't think all revelations are equally complete or adequate. I agree that for Christians, Christ is the criterion or judge of the revelations embodied in other religions, although I have nothing to add to the discussion of this point which has already taken place.

II

I'm still not satisfied with where we've left the word and the idea "religion." Religion still puzzles me, even after our review of options. As St. Augustine said about time, I think I know what religion means until I try to say so. Now I'd like to try to say so.

Revelation, as we've said, is the liberating self-giving of Ultimate Reality. Religion, I will suggest, is the response of a community to that gift. It has both ritual and pietistic components. It has a narrow and conventional reference, which I shall describe as *cultic:* liturgy, prayer, theology, ethics. But it finally includes everything that you do. It has a broad penumbra that I shall call *cultural.* We have often heard lately that theater and art too can be channels of divine communication, and I believe it. Religion has always had a cultural as well as cultic sense. In fact in one of the two places when the word is read in the New Testament, we read, "Religion that is pure and undefiled before God and the Father is this: to visit orphans and widows in their affliction and to keep one's self unspotted from the world" (James 1:27). Not cultic action but worldly action is involved.

We ought to use the word "religion," I believe, with its focus on the narrow cultic, liturgical, pietistic meaning, but also with an awareness of this large cultural penumbra. Religion is the work of a finite and sinful historical community in response to God's liberating, self-giving revelation. The possibility of distortion is always present in religion, the Christian religion as well as any other. Like Professor Carman, I am restive with the dismissal of religion as unfaith, even of the "pickled" variety. That idea doesn't do justice to the genuine if partial transparence of every religion to the power of God. On the other hand, I am unwilling to speak about any religion without qualification as a means of grace.

I should finally want to stand where I think Paul Tillich does on this issue. I should like to have heard more about Tillich's work on religion in John Carman's paper. Tillich holds that every human enterprise is grounded in revelation, and that "original" revelation is both conserved and distorted by a priestly religious tradition. From time to time the distortions are purified. Tillich identifies three corrective forces: mystics who transcend religion, philosophers who subject it to rational criticism, and prophets who criticize it in the name of the original revelation itself: "Thus saith the Lord." The Old Testament provides the archetypical example of this latter process; and the strife goes on forever, since, as we have learned, dogma, structure, and power are both necessary and corrupting.

All talk of distortion and purification implies a basis for judgment. For Christians, Jesus the Christ is the final revelation, wholly transparent to the divine ground. He provides the norm for evaluating the faithfulness to God's revelation in every religion—beginning with our own. "Judgment begins with the household of God" (1 Peter 4:17).

Measured by that canon, all religions, including the Christian, fall short in some respect. But in some respect it is entirely conceivable that other religions might be more adequate than the Christian religion in providing for human welfare as Christ defines that. We can learn from other religions and enrich ourselves from them. At the same time, I would hope other religions could learn from ours and enrich themselves.

III

One more thing. In our discussion at this conference, we have identified two phases in the history of the relation between Christianity and other religions: triumphalism and the present era of good—or at least better—feeling and dialogue. There are several other periods in that history: one of almost complete lack of contact, in the early Middle Ages, and before that, during the first few centuries, one where Christianity was weak and oppressed. Triumphalism was not a remote possibility. In those years, Christians bore witness to their faith, often at the cost of their lives; and, intellectually speaking, they reached out for the highest and best expression of Hellenistic life. I refer to the development of Logos Christology. The meaning of Logos was transformed in that process, but the Christian faith was enriched. It is true that the other religions of that era faded during those centuries. I do not think that such a fate is a necessary component of the process. Those religions were apparently not adequate to the needs of the age. But in our day, other faiths are strong. Can we not mutually reach out to the highest and best in each other's religion? transform it? be enriched by it? Humankind will be well served by the process. And we could afford to leave the outcome in God's hands.

9

Defining Religion from Within

David F. K. Steindl-Rast

Professor Carman has set the concept of religion in its historic and linguistic context in a very erudite, clear, and thought-provoking manner. When I first read his paper with a view to commenting on it, I found myself saying to myself, "Right on! That's it! Good! Fine!" No matter how much I feel the correctness of his analysis, such comments do not make a particularly interesting or helpful response. Fortunately, however, Professor Carman gave to all of us, at the end of his paper, a challenge when he raised a very important question. His question is really a three-fold one, and I quote:

What is the appropriate setting to consider the "Christian church in a religiously plural world?" What is the religious situation in which such thinking must take place and what notion of religion, if any, is relevant to that theological reflection?

The basic question is one of terminology: "What notion of religion, if any, is relevant?" The next question is one of setting or context in which to consider the Christian church in a religiously plural world. Finally, it is necessary to deal with the religious situation in which we live as we struggle with the challenge of religious pluralism in our time. I will try to give my own response to this triple question. But I invite each one of you to give your own response, because these questions are addressed to all of us. Each one of us has to give an answer to these questions from a personal point of view. After all, that is the only place from which we can start, where we are. But it seems only fair that I tell you clearly where I find myself standing as I attempt to answer these questions.

First of all, I am attempting an answer to this question as a member of our human family at a decisive point in history, a juncture which Professor Wilfred Smith has characterized as "the moment in which the human society must become a human community." Like all of us, I am searching for a source of unifying energy that will overcome the self-destructive tendencies from which our human family is suffering. Even though religious dissension, religious wars, and religious persecutions stand out as glaring examples of these self-destructive tendencies, it is my conviction that the religious energy animating these phenomena is, paradoxically, the only force that could bring us together as a human community. My basic stance is simply that of a member of the human family in this crucial situation.

I give my answer also as a monk; that means as someone professionally (yes, for better or for worse—professionally) engaged in the religious quest. In fact, I have come to the dialogue between religions by being a monk. I became acquainted with other religions by meeting other monks. And I got the key to dialogue between religions from the experience of a deep unity with monks of other traditions. There was no question on either side that we had much more in common with one another, say, Buddhist or Hindu monks and Christian monks, than each one of us with our co-religionists who were not monks. Across all the differences in cultic forms and doctrinal formulations, we were simply one in our deepest religious quest. And that was a very important starting point.

I give my answer, however, as a Christian monk, and that means that I put my trust in Christ and in his Good News of salvation. Salvation means to me liberation from alienation in all its different forms. I put my faith and trust in Christ as the great Together in whom all alienation from self, from others, and from God is overcome. My Christian faith is not a barrier separating me from any other religious stance but rather a response uniting me with all other religious responses. This is what it means to me to be a Catholic Christian. For "catholic" means all-embracing.

As a Benedictine monk, I stand in a tradition that is truly catholic in this full sense. Benedictines, after all, antedate the Reformation by a thousand years. We have no axes to grind. Everybody is welcome in a Benedictine monastery; everybody feels at home. In all those 1500 years we have never produced a particularly polemical theologian. That might also say something about the way in which I am tackling Professor Carman's questions. In the last analysis, I have to speak for myself and to offer my own personal answer. But I do feel a great responsibility to the tradition in which I stand. I am quite conscious of having been invited not for my personal merits, but as representing a particular tradition. With sincere conviction I make every effort, not only in this context, but in general, to live and speak out of this tradition. The response I am attempting comes from someone conscious of his roots in our common human heritage and in the catholic Christian, Benedictine monastic tradition.

I am happy to be rooted in this tradition, but I make also a very important distinction between being rooted and being stuck! When you look at a tree that has not yet brought forth its leaves, you are never quite sure whether it is really rooted and alive or merely stuck in the ground. You have to wait until it brings forth new leaves. *New* leaves. That is the point. Rootedness in a tradition, no matter how ancient, will prove its vital strength by producing something genuinely new. The proof that an individual or a group is truly rooted in tradition is their venturesomeness into new grounds, their readiness to go across ever new thresholds of growth.

Having set the scene in this way and having admitted where I stand, I would like now to attempt an answer to Professor Carman's question concerning the position of the Christian church and its message in a world of religious pluralism. Following the three aspects of this question, I propose to explore (1) what terminology we should decide to employ, (2) what setting seems appropriate for facing the challenge of religious pluralism, and (3) what significance emerges from the religious crisis situation in which we find ourselves.

One of the basic questions raised at this symposium was whether or not we should use the term "religion" at all. Although Professor W. C. Smith has argued persuasively for eliminating the term from our vocabulary altogether, I personally would prefer to use a more pragmatic approach. No decree will succeed in purging a living language. People will continue to use the term "religious" anyway, so we might as well try to clarify its meaning and use it intelligently. With Frederick Streng I find that "religious" as an adjective works, while "religion" as an abstract noun leads us astray. Thus I prefer to use the term "religious" and make the best of it.

What, then, do we mean when we use the term "religious" in daily language. You have been using it. What did you mean? We speak, for instance, of someone doing something religiously. What does this imply? Well, first of all, it seems to refer to a certain faithfulness, a certain persistence. But doing something religiously implies more than mere persistence. It implies dedication. When we jokingly speak of someone as religiously reading the *Daily News* after lunch, what strikes us funny is the disproportion between that person's dedication and the lack of meaning in the object of that dedication. We assume that normally one will do with religious dedication only something meaningful. The term "religious" on the part of the subject relates to the notion of meaning on the part of the object. We do religiously what we find meaningful.

When I say "meaning," I have to be very careful to stress that we are concerned here with something different from "purpose," even though in our sloppy everyday language we tend to confuse these two terms. Yet, when you ask yourself how you respond in a situation in which you have to accomplish a purpose and how you respond in a situation in which something becomes meaningful to you, you find that you make two entirely different inner gestures. When it is a matter of acting purposefully, everything depends on your taking things in hand, manipulating them, controlling them, grasping the situation, so that you can use it to accomplish your purpose. When it is a matter of something becoming meaningful to you, you find yourself using expressions like, "It swept me off my feet," "It did something to me," "It really moved me deeply," "It knocked me over"—all these idiomatic expressions present you as passive. Meaning happens to us, meaning is appreciated by us when we *give* ourselves from our heart to whatever it is that we encounter. Purpose demands that we grasp and manipulate things. Obviously, purpose and meaning are not opposed to one another, but complementary. The give-and-take of purpose and meaning should flow as easily as our breath in a happy, healthy life. But we are breathless, because we forget to breathe in. We are so preoccupied with purpose that we fail to give ourselves to meaning.

We are fear-ridden. That is why we turn into manipulators. We dare not give ourselves to the adventure of life. We try to keep things under control. Life is adventure. It involves risk, but in our fearfulness we tend to settle for boredom. All the more we shrink from the ultimate adventure of religious faith and tend to settle instead for dogmatism, moralism, and other areas in which we can manipulate things. Still, the longing for meaning burns in our hearts and will not be quenched so easily. To be human means to live in a world made up of things and meaning. But what ultimately matters to us are not things; it is meaning. What we call our religious quest points somehow toward an ultimate meaning of human existence.

It is my contention that the religious quest is universal because it is the quest for meaning, and without meaning in life we cannot be happy. If there is one thing we can affirm with conviction of any human being who ever lived or will live, it is the desire for happiness. We all want to be happy. What constitutes happiness certainly differs from one person to the next. Maybe no two people will agree in what makes them happy. But we do know that the things we usually associate with happiness in our culture—health, possessions, status —do not ultimately make for happiness. For we all know people who have everything one would need to be happy and who still are miserable. And we know other people who lack all the things that are thought to make one happy and who have nevertheless found true happiness, namely, peace of heart. They have found meaning. The difference between happy and unhappy people is that the former find meaning, even in suffering, while for the latter the many things they could enjoy remain meaningless. What makes the difference is meaning. Our thirst for meaning cannot be quenched until we somehow turn in openness toward the very Source of Meaning. In whatever way we experience this turning, it is the basic religious gesture. Seeing, then, that the quest for happiness is universal and that happiness hinges on meaning, we realize that the religious quest, the quest for ultimate meaning, must also be universal.

To make sure we are not dealing with mere abstractions, let me give you two examples of typical experiences in this quest. The first corresponds to what Abraham Maslow has called the Peak Experience; the second may be called the Agony of Faith. I offer these illustrations mostly to suggest similar experiences in your own life. It is by focusing on your personal experience in your own religious quest for meaning that you will begin to understand from within what we are trying to explore here.

When I invite you to focus on a Peak Experience of your own, this need not be one of those rare peaks we reach once in a lifetime. Remember rather one of those little peaks that stand out from the plain of our daily routine as somewhat elevated moments in which something touches our heart with meaning. After all, an ant hill is also a peak. It doesn't have to be Mt. Everest. Remember, for instance, the moment when that squirrel comes over to the bench where you are sitting. You look at one another and for one split second, just as the little creature takes a peanut from between your fingers—everything makes sense. Everything? Yes, everything. What happens here?

All that seems to have happened is that a squirrel, sitting there on its haunches "like a small grey coffee pot" twitches its tail and makes off with a peanut. Why should life and death and everything make sense to you for one moment in the flash of this experience? What paradoxical disproportion between cause and effect! No one gave you the answer to all your questions. No, but for one moment you drop the questions, and the answer is here. Most other times it is the question that prevents the answer from getting through to you. You are so busy asking questions that you have no ears for the answer. Then this little squirrel hopped across the way and induced you somehow to say, "Yes! "—to this tiny part of reality. But this was a special kind of "yes"—an unconditional "yes." When we say an unconditional "yes" to the smallest part of reality, we have said "yes" to all of reality, down to the very Source of reality. We are in communion with Ultimate Reality and for that moment everything makes sense. We are no longer trying to grasp and to distinguish. We just rest in meaning.

To make sure that we go beyond a *Reader's Digest* sunset glow of religious experience, I suggest you focus now on another kind of experience, on another pole of the same religious encounter with meaning. We might call it the Agony of Faith. It happens that people who thought of themselves as genuinely religious for a long time are suddenly confronted with something in life that seems totally absurd. You hear people say, "Oh, I was a very religious person for fifty years until my husband died. And he died such a terrible death. If God can do such a thing, that's not a God to believe in," or something like that. It is a tremendously tragic thing. Surely, one cannot make any personal judgments at all in a situation like that. Objectively looking at the situation you can say, "Well, God groomed and prepared this person for maybe fifty years for that one moment of making *the* religious gesture, making *the* religious act." That act is to say "Yes" with a grateful heart, even when we cannot understand, when everything seems totally absurd. The very word "absurd" gives the whole situation away, because it means, literally, "absolutely deaf." When we say that something is absurd, we have really made a statement about ourselves. We have said, "I am absolutely deaf to what this situation wants to say to me." There is only one alternative to absurdity, and that is to be obedient.

Ob-audiens, from which the word "obedient" comes, means

thoroughly listening: With the ear of my heart I listen so attentively to the given circumstances that they reveal to me the meaning they embody as a symbol embodies its significance. This kind of listening presupposes a basic attitude of gratefulness. The first thing that the given circumstances tell me is that they are given. I live in a given world. I am faced with a given reality. Everything is gift and deep in my heart I know that the only appropriate response is gratefulness. Gratitude expresses trust in life. It is life-affirming. Fear is life-denying. It brings about the threat from which it shrinks. You can say "thank you" only because you trust in the giver. The person who first looks to see what is inside the package and *then* says, "Thank you," is not really the grateful person. To say, "Thank you," before you unwrap your gift—that is gratitude.

Gratefulness is the courageous "yes" to a given reality, the same "yes" in which we recognized the basic religious gesture in the Peak Experience and in the Agony of Faith. But in the context of gratefulness it becomes more obvious why our happiness should depend on this "yes." We tend to think that the happy people are grateful because they got what they like. In reality it is the grateful people who are happy because they like what they got. They like it because they trust in life and would rather be surprised than reduce life's abundance to the measure of their own limited expectations. This means adventure. The religious "yes" is not a passive "yes." The gratefulness it implies is not a passive attitude. We show ourselves grateful by rising to the challenge of life. This is sometimes dramatic, often painful, always risky.

The context in which this religious key experience takes place is always a historic context because our lives unfold in time and space. It makes a difference at what time in your life, at what time in human history, a given event happens. It makes a difference where a religious experience takes place, or where a religious community settles. Someone even wrote an interesting book about the geographic conditions under which different religious developments take place. There is such a thing as the geography of religion. Time and space shape our religious experience. All the more so does the sociological context in which it arises. It makes all the difference, for instance, whether your key religious experience takes place in a patriarchal or in a matriarchal society. Today Christians are finding out what happens when the patriarchal props are pulled out from under a proclamation of the Good News formulated in predominantly patriarchal language. The underlying shift is a cultural one, but the religious experience necessarily occurs in a particular cultural context. The religious experience by which one appropriates the Good News is no exception. The historic, geographic, sociological, cultural context specifies the religious experience and gives it a particular shape and coloring. But the religious experience as such, the encounter with Ultimate Meaning, lies deeper.

It is from this angle that we might approach Professor Carmans's second question, the question of setting in which to consider the Christian church in a religiously pluralistic world. If our concern is with externals—important externals though they be—the proper setting for our questioning will lie within the special domain of comparative religion, of theology, church diplomacy, even the domain of geography and history. It will be a matter for scholars in these fields. But if we go deeper, if we penetrate to the very core of the religious experience, we are dealing with existential concerns of every human being. We are dealing with our common human quest for meaning and that concerns everyone of us personally. The proper setting for questions arising on that level is no longer the domain of scholars in various fields. When the question concerns our encounter with Ultimate Meaning, the only proper setting is the human heart.

Your heart is the organ for meaning. Just as our eyes perceive light and our ears perceive sound, so it is with the heart that we perceive meaning. When I speak of the heart, I am using this term in its biblical sense. What the Bible calls the heart is not merely the seat of our emotions, but that tap root of our being where intellect, will, and emotions are still one and undivided. The lover who says, "I will give you my heart," speaks of the heart in the biblical sense, the heart as the core of the whole human person. Every genuine response to meaning comes from the heart in this sense. On its deepest level the question of relating our Christian faith to the religious experience in other traditions is a question addressed to your own heart.

We do not often face the issues that flow from Professor Carman's emphasis on the proper setting for exploring religious pluralism. Since it is a matter of conflicting religious convictions—conflicting at least on the surface—I ask you: What then is the basis for your conviction that the Bible is true? Is it tradition? Do you believe because tradition tells you so? Well, then, what makes you believe in tradition? Is it the Bible? What is the basis for your conviction that the Bible is true? Is it theology? Why should we trust the theologians? Is it the church? What makes you trust in the church? Have you ever asked yourself these questions? What is the ultimate basis for our religious convictions? I can only find one answer. It is the personal experience of our heart. Your heart finds this particular expression of faith meaningful. Your heart finds meaning in the commitment to this given tradition, to this given church, to the Bible, to a particular theological view. Your heart has an insight that leads to this conviction, and on the strength of this conviction you dare to commit yourself. But this turns all these questions back to you, to each one of us personally. We cannot excuse ourselves by saying, "Well, it's tradition," or "Well, it's church authority," or "Well, it's this or that." It's my personal conviction, and I have to stand up for it.

We must face the fact that our religious conviction is based on our personal religious experience, or else it has no foundation at all. Does this open the doors wide for religious individualism? Not at all. Notice that I am using the term "personal" when speaking about the religious experience. When we use the term "individual" we focus on what separates one from others. What makes one a person, on the other hand, is interrelatedness with others. One's personal religious experience normally takes place in relationship to a religious community. It is difficult to say what comes first, one's belonging to a religious community or one's personal religious experience. The two are closely interrelated. It is within a religious community that we are presented with that which becomes ultimately meaningful to us.

For a Christian, the religious key-experience is an encounter with the risen Lord. If you can say, "I have met the Risen Lord, and I have committed myself to him," there is no question: You are a Christian. If you cannot say that you have ever met him, you are excused from being a Christian. How could you make a choice for him if you have never met him? And you meet the risen Lord, normally, somehow in the Christian community. But just as in the Gospel accounts, the risen Lord always vanishes from our sight just when we recognize him "in the breaking of bread" (Luke 24:31). We can never pin his presence down. Yet, we do encounter him within the community of believers. His presence touches my heart and my heart responds to this encounter which gives meaning to my life. The community provides the context. But it is in the heart that God's self-disclosure takes place. This is possible because, as Pascal so clearly saw, the human heart infinitely surpasses what is merely human.

In whatever community this experience takes place, in whatever context the heart finds meaning, this religious key experience is always a confrontation with truth. As soon as we discover what confrontation with truth implies, we have found the clue to a unifying view of religious pluralism. As long as we think of truth primarily as something of which we take possession, and exclusively focus on this aspect, truth will be divisive. But look what really happens when you are confronting truth. Isn't it rather that truth takes possession of you? You give yourself to the truth at least as much as you take hold of it. And truth, like reality, is one. Particular truths are partial truths. But a heart that gives itself to the truth gives itself to the whole truth. When we give ourselves courageously to the truth which is one, we are one. If we have had the religious experience in one given context, we know what it means in any religious context to say "yes" to ultimate reality.

This leads us to the final part of Professor Carman's question, namely, to the religious situation in which this answer must take place today. I am convinced that all of us are standing at a new threshold in the history of religions, a threshold at which something very important is happening. The dividing lines no longer run vertically, as it were, between the different religious traditions. Those are, at any rate, no longer the essential dividing lines. They merely mark distinctions between different expressions of an underlying unity. Variety is the splendor of that unity. But the real, painful dividing line runs, so to say, horizontally through each of the different religious traditions. It is the dividing line between those whose religious commitment is inclusive, because they give themselves to the truth, and those whose religious commitment is exclusive, because they think of the truth as something of which one takes possession.

There are, nowadays, inclusive and exclusive Buddhists, and there are inclusive and exclusive Christians, Muslims, and everything else you can name. And all the inclusive (or, if you want, catholic, with a lower case "c") Muslims, Hindus, Buddhists, Christians in the whole world are one. They know that they are one, and acknowledge that they are one. Divisions arise from those whose notion of truth is exclusive. They, too, are to be found in all the different religious traditions. Their exclusiveness separates them even from the "catholics" within their own tradition. This painful dividing line between "catholics" and exclusivists cuts even through the very heart of the Roman Catholic Church.

What does this mean for the Christian church today? I can compare the situation only to what is described throughout the Acts of the Apostles in the Bible. What happens there is that the Christians, who were originally simply a Jewish sect, go beyond Jewish exclusivism in a dramatic way. We can no longer appreciate today what it meant for Jews, for the apostles, for early Christians, to do away with circumcision. Nothing we could do today would in any way be comparable to this radical abolition of exclusivism. The moment they had transcended Jewish particularism, Paul was able to say, "We are the *true* Israel." What happens today, if I see it correctly, is that we are equally invited by God to go beyond exclusivism, Christian exclusivism. Only when we have gone beyond—and this going beyond is a real participation in Christ's death and resurrection—will we recognize that now we are the true kingdom of God. This going beyond is the innermost religious gesture for each one of us personally and for religious communities institutionally.

This means that John Carman's questions will not be solved by discussion, helpful as they may be to many of us. A symposium like this can at best clarify the challenge, as this one has done. Yet, we will have to rise to this challenge not by talking religions, but by being religious. Trusting faith in the one truth that unites us will give us the courage to die to the partial truths that separate us. This is the challenge that this conference and specifically Prof. Carman's paper has put before us. Each one of us will have to rise personally to this challenge.

PART THREE

A RESPONSE

10

An Historian of Faith Reflects on What We Are Doing Here

Wilfred Cantwell Smith

(Unlike other contributing participants, Professor Smith was asked to come to the conference not with a prepared presentation but rather to speak at the conclusion of the gathering on the basis of his observations during the symposium. The following report is reconstructed from a taped recording of his remarks.)

In Islamic history, I have on occasion argued, the most exciting chapter is the one that is currently in the process of being written. It is the most important as well as the most problematic, the most open, the most ambiguous. This has always been the case. Islamic history has been going on now for fourteen centuries, and each of those centuries as it came along was new, dynamic, uncertain, groping, creative, a strange mixture of divine initiative and human response, and human lack of response, and of a wide array of human initiatives. Every generation, it has been said, makes its own decisions. One could add that every generation makes its own mistakes, wrestles with its own problems, and bequeaths to the future its own particular contributing background.

The same is, of course, true in the Hindu case also; only in that instance there have been some thirty-five centuries or more, rather than fourteen. Every one has been different. Each

century of Hindu life has been distinct, not only from the other
centuries of Hindu life, but also from the same centuries, in
each case, of Muslim life or whatever. Not, of course, totally
different. There has been continuity, of which we have heard
much; as well as variety, of which we have heard much. The
religious life of Hindus in any given century has been in some
ways the same as, and in some ways different from, the religious life of Hindus in other centuries and the contemporane-
ous life of other communities in that particular one. Beyond
this, of course, terms like "Hindus," "Muslims," "centuries,"
are enormous oversimplifications. We toss them off as if we
knew what each meant, and as if it were legitimate (maybe it
slightly is) to sum up so glibly so much that is complex.

Obviously, similar observations pertain to Christians. To be
a Christian is to be a member of the Christian Church, which is
something that not only has a history but is a history. To be a
Christian means to participate in the ongoing life of a community in motion.

"To be a Christian" specifies the process in which one par-
ticipates; it specifies also, to some degree, the way in which
one lives in that particular process. It has been mentioned that
the terms "religion"/"religious," and this is certainly the case
also for "Christian" and the like, may be used either as nouns
or as adjectives; and we have heard something also about the
adverbial use. The adverbial is perhaps the most challenging
of these: to try to live Christianly from moment to moment is
that which most teases us, and that at which we are least good,
but that than which perhaps nothing is more important.
Clearly, this kind of observation applies to all human beings.
The human person is an historical creature whose life is what it
is because, in significant part, of its historical setting and the
transition in which it is involved. The human being is also, of
course, a social person; and also a God-related person. The
human condition is that of living in motion through particular
times in relation to other persons and in relation to God.

I have been asked to comment on this conference. It strikes
me, first of all, as a particular moment in Christian Church
history. It is not the most important moment in that history of

this century, nor even of this year; yet it is not the least important, either, by any means. I should guess that some sense of the unusual significance of this moment through which we have been living has probably struck most of us.

I myself find it significant, not only because of what has been said by the speakers—I have been impressed by the papers that I have heard—but also, and in some ways first, by the audience that has gathered. Mission secretaries, townspeople, clergy, academics, layfolk, students, religious followers, religious inquirers, religious observers: A great company of us have gathered, and have participated with engagement. Would it be too strong to aver that we have all, or almost all, taken part with a remarkable degree of excitement? Certainly, something has stirred us. Some few, I feel, have been taken aback at what they have seen going on here. We have heard certain expressions of perplexity or of concern. That is fine. Not everything that has happened in Church history has been or will be good. Not all Christians have agreed, by any means, as to which things were good and which were not. And if I be at all right that this occasion is significant, then anything as significant as this will certainly elicit differing responses from various Christians. Some few, then, have as I say been concerned; most, I think, have been excited; and all, I guess, have been impressed.

Those of us who are academics have been impressed by the public character of the occasion. Ideas with which we have been accustomed to concern ourselves in our studies, we find here moving out into the marketplace, as it were: being criticized and probed and reacted to, we find, by a much wider circle than our small intellectualist coterie. For example, the seminars yesterday: Unfortunately, I was not able to attend all of them; unfortunately, none of you was either. But I did try to attend a few more than one, because of my role as an observer. And once again, I was struck by the excitement with which people who, I should guess, a week ago, and certainly a decade ago, would never have imagined that they would be *engagés* in such affairs, were discussing with a Buddhist or a Muslim certain Christian problems, and were excited or teased or puzzled or illuminated by the answers that they got. This is surely striking. Most of us have felt that something is indeed astir.

It is not, of course, the first time that members of differing religious communities have gathered together. Four hundred years ago last January, the Mughal emperor Akbar in India (one of the perhaps two greatest rulers that India has produced in its long history, a man who is said to have conquered the world and then to have been restless that he could not understand it) took time off from his military and administrative and other duties to set up what he called "a house of worship" (*'ibādat khānah*) in his capital at Agra. To it he invited first of all representatives of the various schools of Islamic thought (following perhaps Dr. Price's delightful story about theologians?) to carry on debates and discussions in his presence. He did so because he was entranced by the issues at stake. After a while, however, he found this was not as satisfying as he had hoped, and he then heard about some Christian missionaries away off in Bengal, people from foreign lands across the sea; accordingly, he sent for them inviting them to come and to join in these weekly "seminars." Presently other communities too were asked to participate. There was lively interchange.

A further four hundred and more years even before that there are interesting accounts of comparable occasions in Islamic history. I think, for instance, of a particular Muslim traveller from Spain who turned up in Baghdad, a much more sophisticated capital city than he was accustomed to. He has left his record of his dismay in finding discussions going on in which Islam, his own form of faith, was being challenged and discussed and put alongside other religious positions, as represented by spokesmen of other communities, in a give-and-take that led him to pen some entrancing pages in his diary.

Again, in medieval Spain we have what has been called the "trilogue," with Muslims, Jews, and Christians talking with each other seriously. We may rather use for that occasion the term "tetralogue," if one adds the philosophers as a fourth group who participated in, and in part mediated, that discussion. Coming down to more recent times, as Gerald Anderson reminded us, for the last few decades the notion of "dialogue" has been on the agenda of the Vatican, the World Council, and other Christian groups. It has become a common concept and a fairly common occurrence. Not only do groups from differing communities talk to each other; they talk *with* each other about common problems—what one might call "colloquy." These are occasions set up exclusively to bring to bear on common modern human issues the combined wisdom—or diversified wisdom or, anyway, juxtaposed wisdom—or differing religious communities.

What we have been witnessing here is, I suggest, somewhat different from all this, past or present. This occasion was taken at Christian initiative to deal with a Christian problem; to try to solve a problem of which Christians have of late become increasingly aware and to which increasingly sensitive. It may be called, if you like, the dilemma or the paradox or, as Minor Rogers put it to us, the *kōan* of Christians; that is, the puzzling, teasing question to elicit humility and ultimately to give enlightenment and to generate wisdom: the dilemma of universality and particularity. What is striking here is that a group of Christians concerned with a specifically Christian problem decided to invite members of other religious communities to help us solve our dilemma. We found ourselves involved with an issue that was in some sense, at least for the sensitive, tearing us apart, as it were; and it occurred to some that maybe a Jew, a Muslim, a Hindu, a Buddhist could help us solve our problem.

That was striking enough. That has not often happened. Equally striking were the facts that they came, and that they *did* help.

It is a fact that their contributions have illuminated for Christians a Christian problem. Still more striking was that this was seen to be taking place. We have sat through an occasion in which we have seen ourselves being helped on a specifically Christian issue by inviting and receiving the concern of fellow human beings—persons, to use an old and I think outdated phrase "from the outside."

Our Christian dilemma can be set forth in a variety of ways.

One way is to speak of loyalty to the traditions, to Christ, to the salvation that the Church has known, on the one hand, and on the other hand of sensitivity to the feelings of others and to the truth and the increasingly recognized revelation and divine activity in the life of others. A more general way is to speak, as has been done, of the relation of universality to particularity. Still another way is to speak of the dilemma between the theological and the moral. Our inherited theological imperatives seem to push us in one direction, while our inherited moral imperatives, equally Christian, equally central, equally inescapable, push us in the other, towards more brotherhood and concern, towards less destructive and alienating activities, less digging of gulfs between "us" and "them." Or one may speak of a dilemma between our internal and our external affairs. However one puts the problem, I believe that it speaks well for the Christian conscience that it has been troubled by this paradox. It would be too bad if the Church were not nowadays kept awake at night by the at times terrible dilemma that is presented if we settle glibly for either of two seeming alternatives: of giving up, on the one hand, a central thrust of the whole of Christian history, or, on the other hand, of giving up a clear and surely inescapable moral obligation to other people. We cannot choose between loving God, as Christians feel that God is revealed, or loving our neighbor.

It speaks well for the Christian conscience that it is troubled. And it is dramatic that we should choose this present way of attempting to alleviate this problem. It is dramatic also to find, I am suggesting, that this new way does, in fact, work. The Church has here taken a bold step and it turns out to be one that has carried us very far forward.

We have mentioned the speakers and the participants in the conference. The organizers too, clearly, have played a crucial role, and one could say many things in applause of their patterning. In particular I was struck by the ingenious device of their having the theological statement responded to by people of other communities and the comparativist's statement responded to by theologians. It would have been more obvious, and in certain ways it would perhaps have been easier for all concerned, to have the theological paper commented upon by theologians, and the comparativist paper commented upon by a comparative panel, with responses from diverse forms of faith. Yet it was done the other way. This is one of the things that has been delightful. Surely also it has been important. It is no minor fact that a theologian knew that what he was writing on his topic would be read by, and would be publicly commented upon by, Jews and Hindus and Muslims and Buddhists. Similarly, vice versa: It was important that the comparativist—and this is equally novel—knew that his statement must be conceived in such a way that it would command the intelligibility, at least, and respect, not merely of other academics, but of theologians. Such matters have been illustrative of, and have underlaid, the fertile and exciting quality of our time together.

Surely no one but was stimulated by hearing Dr. Borowitz, a Jew, calling on the Christian universalist to be cautious: "Hold on there, now! You're becoming too generous; you're letting go too readily a precious and non-dispensable quality in any religious community. Think about it." We did think about it; and thought also about the fact that it was he who was making this point. Insofar as Christians may have been surprised at this, it is perhaps a measure of the distance that we have yet to go in being educated. I shall not embarrass the others by commenting on their statements, except to say that I imagine that many in our group were struck to find, in listening to Dr. Fazlur Rahman, Dr. Seshagiri Rao, Dr. Mahinda Pallhawadana, how humane they were as they discussed our Christian problems with us. Again, if this was in any fashion surprising, it is a matter for enormous embarrassment and repentance. Yet in some ways I think it is the case that the Christian Church has yet to discover, in any serious and profoundly theological fashion, how human, as it were, everyone else is. Christians are enabled to be human through Christ; but the faith of other people enables them equally.

And at the same time Christians discovered that our problem as Christians, although it is a Christian problem, is not merely that but is a human problem, that as became more vivid during the course of our time together, the dilemma between universality and particularity—or the fact that each of us lives in a particular time and place, yet in relation to eternity —characterizes not merely us, now, in the Christian Church, but all people at all times. It is well worth our getting together to talk about this because we can, in fact, help each other.

Some of those who have spoken have paid me the compliment of commenting on some of the ideas that I have put forward in my published writings over the years. I am not going to pay myself the compliment of taking time to comment on this; with one exception. This is the issue of whether it be "religion" that we have in common. Two spokesmen have already selected, and I therefore perhaps may also select, the remark in John Carman's paper that "it does not ultimately matter what concept one chooses for designating that quality that we all have in common. The important thing is to recognize that we have it." Now I agree so deeply with virtually everything in Dr. Carman's paper, including this point, that I do not in any sense wish to argue the matter. Yet I think that it might perhaps be worthwhile to proffer this suggestion: namely, that what Christians, Buddhists, Hindus, Muslims, Jews have in common is perhaps not religion but humanity. It is worth pondering that the Christian, the Muslim, and the others are ways, not of being religious, but of being human. It does, also, matter to some degree how we can conceptualize these things. The issue is not disposed of so easily as this, by any means; nonetheless, there is a question here as to whether or not we conceptualize "the religious" as something over and above or special, added to our common humanity in some cases. This is a solution toward which the secular history of the recent western world has tended to push us. It is possible rather to conceptualize matters in such a way as to recognize irreligious secularity as a pathological aberration, with our being Christian, and Jews' being Jewish, and Hindus' being

Hindu, and Muslims' being Islamic, as a central and integral component of our all being human.

I profoundly believe, and imagine that everyone in this room does also (though Professor Palihawadana would have to phrase this in a different vocabulary; but he is generous and very astute, and I think that even he will allow it)—I profoundly believe that being human means being involved with God, or with the one whom we call God, and that this is not an additive in human history but the very foundation, both of our humanity and of history itself.

Over against this form of universality, I was particularly taken by a suggestion of Professor Carman that there is a specific historical ingredient, touching on this issue, in the differential relation of Christians with Jews and Muslims on the one hand, and with Hindus and Far Easterners on the other, because we have shared a common boundary with the former groups, and have been involved with them over the centuries in intimate and in some cases, of course, disastrous ways. The particular relations of Christians with Jews and of Christians with Muslims have had an historical dimension and continue to have; it would be jejune to forget that. The "religious" collisions and conflicts, and worse, that have arisen and that have vitiated our relations in these two cases are certainly special. Compared with those involvements, a question as to what it be that Chinese and Christians or Hindus and Christians have in common is hardly the same. In those cases these issues can be thought of as much more conceptualist or philosophical. More work must be done at this level. My own personal view has been that the historical interinvolvement of the entire world in this realm is probably much greater than we have traditionally been aware. Nonetheless those of us who are Christian, in being Christian, are engaged in a human issue, and those of us who are Muslims, in being Muslim, are engaged in a human issue, and so on for Buddhists and others. This, I feel, brings us together.

Yet I do not wish to pursue this particular point here; my comment on this Symposium, rather, is that this kind of issue has been illustrated here, and probably all of us will go away pondering such matters, open to new awareness. It will be an awareness not merely of intellectual issues. As intellectuals, these we may pursue; but we have become open with a new openness of a profoundly human sort, as a result of our gathering.

Religion, I am sure—and Brother David illuminated this for us in a particularly charming way—does not come to us in packaged forms; and the issue is not whether once we unwrap the packages they will all turn out to have the same content. Faith is a much more intimate, dynamic, inseparable component that is ingredient in the life of each of us from day to day, and not merely in our life, but in our ultimate being.

A personalist view of these issues is by no means an individualist one; and it is on that note that I would close. The person is a person through being inter-involved with other persons. And it turns out that we are Christians, those of us who are so, not only in ourselves, but in relation to others on earth. We know this in a way that is much more dramatic than it was fifty years ago, or even fifty hours ago. That new knowledge is something in which I, at least, rejoice, and about which all of us cannot but be excited.

PART FOUR

EXPLORATIONS

Explorations

In planning this symposium, we wanted to have not only a carefully structured program centering on the main theme, but we also wanted to have an opportunity for exploring new themes and unexpected approaches. To accomplish this, we invited participants in the symposium to offer seminars in which they explored themes related to the question of religious pluralism and Christian faith. Some of these seminars were concerned with the teaching of religion or new research on particular topics in philosophy, theology, ethics or history. Some of the leaders of these seminars subsequently wrote papers that made it possible to share the results of their work with those who could not attend personally. This aspect of the symposium we have called "Exploration." Three essays emerged from the seminar work in exploring concerns and insights that grew out of the symposium theme but bringing different perspectives on them.

One of the problems in planning a symposium of this sort is not excluding certain traditions while still avoiding a bewilderingly large and ungainly collection of persons and ideas. The problem was not so much one of fearing sharply differing or critical viewpoints. The papers themselves show the way in which understanding is built and truth perceived in the point and counterpoint of argumentation, even when sharply pursued. Rather it was that blindspots in planning only became evident in the actual work of the symposium itself. For this reason we were very appreciative of the contribution of *Dr. Alfred Krass*, co-editor of *The Other Side*, author of several books on evangelism, and a former missionary of the United Church of Christ in Ghana. His essay, "Accounting for the Hope Which Is in Me," brings to bear the witness of conservative Protestantism with its strong sense of the evangelistic mission

151

of Christianity to those in other religious traditions. This was a voice that needs to be fully and clearly heard as Christians try to resolve in our time the challenge of the particularity and universality of their faith.

In his address Professor Carman spoke of the Jewish and Christian willingness to translate their Scriptures as a witness to their conception of religion and that of human nature which underlies it. Translatability, he argues, is only possible if you assume there is a common humanity that lies behind the bewildering complexity of human religiousness. Translatability from one religious context to another presupposes there is some basis by which human beings may address one another in the name of their ultimate concern that transcends cultural and religious particularity. Such an overarching anthropological presupposition comes to the test when confronted by the difficult task of an actual translator struggling to make the message of his Scripture understandable to others. *Professor John Ross Carter* of Colgate University explores this question in light of translating the Bible into other languages.

One of the oldest ways by which Christians have understood the various kinds of religions has been by the distinction they make between "faith" and "works." Already in the first century, Paul used the distinction between those who sought salvation by works of ascetic piety, legal observance, and ritual performance and those who sought it in the self-abandoning trust of faith. In our own time, Hendrik Kraemer has utilized this distinction in his analysis of religion. However, Christians have always proceeded on the notion that their religion is the only one based on faith, while all the others are seeking for righteousness by works. The modern study of the history of religions has raised important questions as to whether such a distinction can, in fact, be maintained. Certainly the Saivites of India speak eloquently of grace and faith against all works, as seen in *The Tiruvāsagam* of the Tamil poet Mānikkavāsagar and others. But other traditions seem devoid of any notion of grace and understand salvation as the result of the patient accumulation of merit. This has long been a dominant understanding of Buddhism, particularly the Theravada schools. For this reason, we found the seminar by *Professor Mahinda Palihawa-dana* an exploration of great importance. As one standing in the Theravada traditions of Buddhism, he raises the question "Is there a Theravada Buddhist idea of grace?"

Professor Palihawadana had opened this question at the meeting of a learned society during his previous visit to the United States. Now he has brought it to fuller expression in a paper that illuminates this issue out of the texts themselves. His paper is technical in form, being based on detailed analysis and interpretation of some of the great texts of the Theravada Buddhist tradition. These texts were written in Pali and require careful attention to their linguistic form and to the tradition of interpretation in which they stand. Just as he has wrestled with the text, the reader is called to wrestle with a complex issue. But we believe that this effort will be rewarded.

11

Accounting for the Hope That Is in Me

Alfred C. Krass

Persons interested in the theology of mission in modern times are becoming familiar with the application of sociological insights to mission studies. Although anthropology has been the discipline of the social sciences most commonly brought into missiological studies, sociologies of various types have gained increasing attention and usefulness in missiology in recent years.

In theoretical studies, the type of sociology I most often see used is the sociology of knowledge, which stems from the work of the German sociologist Karl Mannheim. In the United States it is Peter Berger who has been chiefly responsible for spreading the use of this type of sociology among Christian theologians. One of Berger's former students, the Catholic theologian Gregory Baum, has recently attempted to apply the insights of the sociology of knowledge to the analysis of the absolute and unique claims of the Christian faith. In dialogue with Charles Forman of Yale University Baum has seen fit to question the validity of the attempt to "go on repeating the absolute claims of New Testament and ancient church teachings at a time when Christian faith has become the established religion of a dominant civilization."[1] Baum says that by so doing one becomes unfaithful to the original meaning of these teachings. This is, Baum says, preserved only when the teachings are spoken by an oppressed minority.

Baum's arguments are extremely germane to the subject of this colloquium on "Christian faith in a religiously plural world." I found myself differing considerably from Baum as I read his dialogue with Forman, even while I have at this colloquium found myself agreeing with most of the arguments put forward by Donald Dawe. This might seem a contradiction, and yet I believe it is not.

It is nonetheless strange to me that I differ so much from Baum, for, like Baum, I "come from a Jewish family" and I am an ordained minister of a Christian church. But unlike him I have no difficulty in proclaiming the church's teaching that "Jesus Christ is Lord" and hoping for the day when every tongue, every race and nation, shall confess him (Phil. 2) and "there shall be one flock, one shepherd" (John 10:16).

Yet it would not be fair for me to outline my views without giving a clear statement of what Baum intends. He is referring to Mannheim's distinction between "ideological" statements and "utopian" ones. In Mannheim's sense ideologies are "interest-laden utterances" of ruling elites. Utopias, on the other hand, are the projections of oppressed minorities. Baum says that the Christian confession of unity under the lordship of Christ started out as a survival cry of a powerless group—it was a utopian cry—but "when the Christian church became the religion of the Roman Empire and later identified itself with Western society, the same doctrinal statements acquired a different meaning." The church's exclusive claims became "a language of power and domination"; in other words they became ideological claims.

Baum therefore calls upon the church to stop making such claims in order to create "theological space for the great world religions." The church will still have a missionary message, Baum feels, but that message will "exercise its salvational power where people are in fact in their cultural environment," by enabling them "to cling more faithfully to the best of their religious tradition and live the full personal and social implications of their religion more authentically."

I must at the outset indicate that, though I differ from Baum in the solution he proposes, I recognize the problem Baum deals with: the association of Christian faith with cultural imperialism. Though I stand in the long train of Christians who have taken the message of Christ to places where it has not previously been heard, I know the history of the missionary movement too well not to recognize its blemishes—its caricatures of the gospel, its outright denials of the faith of Christ crucified. A crucified Lord can—in the hands of dominant elites—become an imperious idol of culture. I am aware of the problems "younger Christians" worldwide have in achieving, as Christians, a sense of cultural authenticity and their liberation from western superiority; I recognize that, in a real way, many of them have become culturally deracinated by virtue of the type of conversion or Christian nurture they have undergone. As one aware of these things I cannot but choose to be involved in movements for the authentic contextualization of Christian theology. I cannot feel anything but remorse for the long marriage between Christian missions and western ethnocentrism (even though I recognize that the marriage, in its grossest form, lasted less than a century; there was a missionary movement long before it and there is today a missionary movement becoming every day freer of it).

Nevertheless, my criticism is that Baum is posing a much more radical challenge to the missionary movement than that it become "culturally sensitive." He is saying that it must reconceive its basic message, that its reading of the New Testament must become "liberated," that it must become able to separate the "utopian context" of the New Testament message from its essential truths and recognize that in calling all people to recognize Jesus as Lord it is not being faithful to the essence of the faith. Baum feels that it is not God's intention that all people become Christians; if we understand God's intention more deeply we will rather *not* ask them to join the church. We must recognize that we are no longer in a survival situation—our faith is culturally dominant, our civilization is dominant. To invite people to become Christian is to seek to absorb them, to destroy their culture. We must therefore reformulate our original message, Baum says, in such a way that it "leaves room for other groups on God's earth." The motto

"Jesus Christ is Lord," understood in an absolute sense, does not leave such space.

I think Baum reads the primitive Christian creed correctly. It is a sweeping claim. It calls for nothing less than conversion to Christ's lordship. Unlike some others, I understand the confession "Jesus Christ is Lord" to be an absolute one. In my interpretive work I constantly tell church groups that the word that is *not* in the confession—"my" or "our"—is the crucial word. The confession is absolute. Like the other New Testament affirmation, "He is Lord of all," it is not substantially less exclusive than the Christ-hymns in Colossians and Philippians. In the minds of the early Christians there was no doubt but that *their* Lord was *the* Lord.

And this is how I, too, heard the message when I was in college, in an exclusive sense. If the Christians I had met there, when I was an agnostic Jew, had been less exclusive, I would have had no trouble with them. But as it was I could not help but see that, no matter how warm and loving and accepting as persons they were, their whole being addressed me with the question: "Will you recognize as Lord the one to whom we have committed ourselves? Will you confess that he is *the* Lord?" They exercised no moral suasion. They were ready to continue their friendship whether I accepted their creed or not. They refused to manipulate me. I had sought them out, not they me. But my question to them—"Why are you so wonderfully different from everyone else around?"—could be answered only by reference to their faith.

The agnostic in me yielded long before the Jew in me did. I came to believe in the reality of God because I saw God alive and powerful in the lives of these disciples of God. But I still kept asking, "Is there not, under God, any other way? Only the way of Jesus? Must it be so exclusive? Could we not accept Jesus, perhaps, as Teacher and Prophet alongside, even as the greatest of, others? Rather than as Lord, Shepherd, High Priest, and King?"

I searched the Scriptures and I saw no other way conformed to the records; it was not just a matter of pruning the "utopian" statements and leaving the essentials. It was a matter of recognizing that either Jesus was who he claimed he was and who his disciples confessed him to be, *or* he was a megolomaniac or a dangerous *poseur*, and his disciples were therefore deceived. Like Schweitzer before me, I encountered a Jesus not reducible to what my age would have had him be.

It was *after* I had accepted this unbending Christ that I first was able to make the historically prior affirmation (which had always earlier struck me as an affront to the modern mind): that *my* people, Israel, was God's chosen people. In both matters it was "the scandal of particularity" that had offended me. But in both cases I found, after that, in his strange economy, God does work through the historically particular, choosing certain people, certain times, certain places for his acts, that those particular selected persons, places, and times become enlarged; God uses them for the transformation of "unvisited" persons, places, and times. In a real way, that which God chooses gains by his choice of it a power of transcendence. (Shall we call this the mystery of Abraham's election: "In thy seed shall all nations be blessed"?)

Theologically this is why the issue does not hang ultimately on the question of "equal justice for all." *God's justice, his justification of all, comes about* neither through "democratic" leveling nor through the divinization of the principle of pluralism but—glory be!—*through his total commitment to the specific in his acts of salvation*. "All get their share," ultimately, but they "proclaim the name of . . . blessed" when they get it. Abraham/Israel/Mary/Christ (and whoever may be the vehicle or vessel) discover themselves to be the *pars pro toto*, the ones chosen by God not for their own sakes but for the blessing he will through them bring to all.

I came to understand this theologically more than a dozen years ago. I came to understand it sociologically—and historically—only in the last year or two. And therefore it's interesting to see how Father Baum and I (quite naturally, I think) part not only theologically but sociologically as well. He looks to Mannheim and the sociology of knowledge; I look to Durkheim and other processual sociologists.

I find the sociology of knowledge a rather thin gruel. Like Baum's theology at this point, it is essentially ahistorical, concentrated on the now, on the present relationships of isolable actors and on groups and peoples whose coherence is traceable to anterior "interests" or to their position in a power survey. The statements they make—their ideologies or utopias—are thus analyzable in terms of the positions they hold or the groups of which they are a part. All truth becomes relative to who the speaker is in the social field, which is conceived of as a gridiron of conflicts and interests.

This method is fundamentally ahistorical, non-processual. It can be applied at any point in time with equal results, for life in this view is basically a power game and power is always divided unequally. Some get more and others have less, some are dominant and others are dominated; the former therefore have "ideologies" and the latter "utopias." What will be different in the next century will be only that the power—and the ideologies and utopias—will be shared around differently.

The sociology of knowledge is a way of figuring out why people talk and think the way they do. Its central teaching is that, within the context of the now, there is a "social" reason for it. I take the sociology of knowledge to be a somewhat useful subdiscipline of sociology, not a surrogate for it. Sociology to me is a larger, historically richer, and processually more analytical discipline. It is historical and cross-cultural; it encompasses the in-depth comparative analysis of a Max Weber as well as the processual analyses of an Emile Durkheim or a Henry Maine.

This larger sociology takes as its object of study not just the small group or the class structure or even the nation-state. It analyzes the social field in terms of the largest possible units or "social bodies" we can find, the broadest form of social life we discover; whole societies, even civilizations have not been beyond its purview, and today it is moving on to sociological study in global perspective.

It does not see the power struggles within a particular nation or society as unimportant but, in its predominantly "civilization-analytic" perspective, these power struggles are seen in a particular light. "Ideologies" and "utopias" may be more similar than they are different: The oppressed group reveals in its utopian projections a civilizational perspective that has much in common with that which its oppressors express through their ideologies. What makes that civilization, with its competing centrifugal and centripetal forces, still one civilization? What differentiates it so much from another (equally internally fragmented) civilization? What place have various movements had in shaping that civilization? What forces are leading to its transformation? What encounters has it had with other civilizations that have led to new breakthroughs?

It is within such a larger canvas that an analysis of Christianity belongs. Christianity cannot adequately be reduced to the level of a party manifesto; to submit it to analysis by Mannheimean sociologists of knowledge is to predetermine its fate: It will be reduced to a much smaller thing than it has in history been.

Only a sociology which takes histories seriously and fully and studies them in civilizational perspective can deal with phenomena as rich as the great world religions or Marxism or western science.

Such a sociology recognizes that Christianity is not just the religion of a particular people but a world-historical phenomenon. The Christian movement has had a very diverse, far reaching, and extensive history. Christian ideas and Christian affirmations have been let loose in world history: They are embodied in various configurations, encased in various institutions; they are constituent elements of various cultural complexes. They have a life of their own. They antedate us as individuals or as churches or as peoples. They are what Durkheim called "social facts," "ways of acting . . . capable of exercising on the individual (or on social bodies) an external constraint, . . . existing in their own right independent of their individual manifestations." We cannot choose, nor can the world, whether they are going to continue to exist.

Just as the world is a different place because the Roman law was once codified, and just as the world is not what it was before the printing press or television was invented, so the world is, in part, what it is today because the Holy Spirit let loose through the apostles in the first century energizing powers and new elements of human consciousness which, taking on a life of their own, have shaped the histories of most of the world's peoples. We cannot start to codify law today as if the Codex Juris Civilis was never promulgated, nor can we deal with communications in the age of Telstar as if Gutenberg had never printed a book. Historical sociology tells us that we don't start from scratch.

In almost every part of our planet, cultures are what they are today in part because there have been and are cheap, mass-produced books and in part because Roman concepts of law have become an almost universal heritage. Similarly Christianity has shaped not only the cultures and civilizations of Europe and the Americas, but other cultures and civilizations as well: Islam and Hinduism and Buddhism; and their ideas—the structures of the consciousness—have been influenced by ideas that are Christian in their origin but have become part of a universal patrimony. Even if all western Christians today were to become devotees of astrology, we could not restore *Kismet* to the position it once held in Islam nor regain for the eclipse its original power in China.

But it is more than just a religious matter. It is inconceivable that either the secular state in India or Mao's China would be what it is today, or that Marxism for that matter would even exist, were it not for the powerful, secularizing ideas of the antisacral Jewish-Christian prophetic tradition or the universalizing influence of Christ's revolutionary teaching concerning kinship; nor would the Marxist paradise be conceivable without Christian millennarianism. These ideas have become embodied in institutions. Their original association with the teachings of Jesus may be something of which the Indians, Americans, and Chinese are unaware, but originally they were tied up with the person of Jesus of Nazareth and the exclusive claim that his disciples made about his sovereignty.

And that is not irrelevant. The past history of present institutions, we must recognize, involved revolution as well as evolution, innovation as well as development. *Krisis* after *krisis* was hammered out on the anvil of history as intolerant visionaries challenged accepted ways with the continual call: "Choose this day whom you will serve." It was this *krisis*, initiated by people associated with the gospel, that removed the fixity of tradition from world historical process and provided the dynamic for many critical transformations.

It would not have happened had the servants of hope doubted that they were servants of the truth, whether that truth was in the realm of theology, physics, or medicine.

I call them, rather uncritically, servants of hope. My point is that whether they were missionaries or imperialists they did not just serve up utopias, nor seek to spread ideologies. They had a vision that transcended their own group's relations to other groups. They felt called to reshape the world according to a vision of its future. It was their eschatology that distinguished them from mere soldiers of fortune. That eschatology could be other-wordly or secularized, but it was revolutionary or it was nothing.

Now they often, as Burgess Carr has so well pointed out, confused what their culture prized with what they had received and threw in the *adiaphora* with the essentials, dubbing all equally "the way." The treasure was not destined to be preserved from earthen vessels. "Teach them to observe all that I have commanded you" became a mandate to impose foreign cultures, even at times by the sword.

But when all is said and done, we must recognize that it was not by a claim that "many paths lead to the top of Mt. Fuji" nor by a fable of five blind men describing an elephant that the Christian dynamic made its presence felt in the histories of the world's peoples. Preferring a Ricci to a Pizarro or a Charlemagne, we must still recognize that what divided even the followers of the liberal Ricci from the Chinese whom Ricci so humbly served was the ability of western Christian science to say "no"—after some false starts—to the dominance of astronomy by sacro-magical interests. Chinese astronomers could not do so. They remained astrologers.

Many missionaries, both before and since Ricci and de Nobili, have stood squarely against the rape of cultures by the servants of the Good News. They have been as offended as is Baum by the suggestion that Christianity should be used as an instrument for the imposition of a technically superior western culture upon nonwestern peoples. Like Ricci they have preferred to see the gospel working as a leaven in nonwestern cultures rather than as a hammer; they wanted it to transform and purify those cultures from within, bringing into being in time distinctively Mandarin or Brahmin forms of Christianity.

One cannot avoid, however, the uncomfortable recognition that both Ricci and de Nobili—and many since—to a great extent failed to achieve this goal. The shortsightedness of Rome was undoubtedly part of the reason, in Ricci's case, but from the viewpoint of a comparative differential sociology we can see in cross-cultural perspective that there was more to the problem than Rome's narrowness: Ricci underestimated the extent to which the whole of Mandarin society was inescapably linked to the divine immanentism of Confucian religion. He thought of certain of the Chinese rites as part of "a religion," which the Chinese could shuck in favor of Christian faiths and rites while maintaining Confucian "philosophy" and culture and Confucian political and social organization (for these were "secular" matters). But that is where Ricci was too much a westerner; he imported the "two swords" doctrine into China. Chinese social and political structure—the examination system, reverence for ancestors, the whole kinship system, and the imperial household—were, and Ricci failed to see this, part of the Confucian immanentist philosophical-theological system. Mao later recognized what Ricci didn't, and he saw that, unless the kinship solidarity was broken and the philosophy dispelled, the new form of social solidarity he sought to bring could not be created.

Therefore sociologists of history recognize that what Weber called "prophetism" came to China not from the legitimate heirs of Judeo-Christian prophecy but from their illegitimate Marxist offspring!

That the challenge to sacro-magical and kinship structures in the end has to come, or else there will be no change, is something Baum would keep us from recognizing. Mao, on the other hand, being no Baumian, did not "leave theological space" for Confucianism (so that the Chinese could "exercise the salvational Power" of Maoism "in their own cultural environment.") He did not tell the Confucians "to cling more faithfully to the best of their religious tradition and live the full personal and social implications of their religion more authentically." He heard another voice, the voice of sine qua non: Without a fundamental challenge to the existing order in the name of a higher—and exclusive—law, all amelioration, all reform, all "influence" would ultimately be of no avail. The break had to be made if there was to be a breakthrough. The sociology of knowledge, however, being non-processual, knows nothing of breakthroughs or transformations, of the formation of civilizations and civilizational complexes, of depth histories. All is a power game, consisting of subordination and superordination. The question of truth is irrelevant to it; ethics are secondary. It is "interests" that count. If a given sociologist of knowledge happens to be democratically inclined, he will recognize that interests are plural. He will seek to "create space" for them. In a doctrine of "pluralism" he will find the required response to the plurality of interests.

To enshrine the doctrine of cultural pluralism at the expense of a fundamental devotion to truth—or to the one who said "I am the Truth"—is to deny the chief lesson of comparative historical sociology: that critical breakthroughs to new levels of consciousness are occasioned by challenges to particularism in the name of that which is held to be universal. The critical breakthroughs in world historical process are precisely the breakthroughs to universality. The "utopian" universalism of the early Christians was thus not an aberration of the central truth of the gospel or something we can explain by social psychology, but an expression of the gospel's central truth. To remove that element, as Baum proposes, is to reduce Christianity to the role of a culture-religion of the Christianized nations.

You can't remove the "arrogance" of Christianity without making it something other than Christianity, no more than you could expect Muslims to remain Muslims were their creed to become: "There are many Gods beside God, but Mohammed was one of their prophets." Radical monotheism is ultimately intolerant of pluralism. When unmixed with grace, monotheism can become totalitarian, even demonic. When, however, it is mixed with the announcement of the forgiveness of sins and the call to repent (Luke 24:47), it is a call to new life, and that life can—must—take many forms. It is also a call to the proclaimers, that they themselves be continually converted, that repentance be a continuing characteristic of the Christian life.

This is thus not to decry pluralism, but simply to refuse to make of it more than what it can be. There need be, in Christian universalism, distinctly cultural incarnations of the one faith, expressions of the faith developed in the context of the contemporary struggles of the people of any area to work out their witness in a culturally and historically relevant and authentic way. But this calls for plural expression of the living, changing universal, not an abandonment of the universal for the plural.

And yet, at the end, I do not want to reject Baum out of hand; what I am saying is that another solution must be found to the problem Baum has tried to deal with: cultural imperialism and triumphalism. For my part, I feel that Charles Forman describes some of that solution quite adequately in calling for an open, listening, dialogical stance vis-à-vis people of other traditions. But his answer is too individualistically oriented fully to satisfy me. I wish Forman had strengthened Baum's sociology rather than accepted it.

What I would have liked to have heard him say would go something like this: "The world you are talking about, Gregory Baum, is on the way out. A world dominated by 'the Christian West' is not one we can expect to see continue much longer. The West has already suffered many setbacks, and, with the crisis of natural resources, seems doomed to suffer many more.

"No one knows what the new world order is going to look like, but one thing is sure: If any part of the world is ill-prepared for it, it is the erstwhile 'Christian West.' Charmed for too long by the comfortable chords of its own praises, it seems unable to recognize that 'western civilization' may not survive the century. No part of the world is less willing to give up its prerogatives for the sake of a new level of social organization, the level of the world's first truly global civilization, than is the West, and unless humankind can move to that new level, survival is really a question."

We must therefore say to the western world, "You who once taught the nations to sing, 'Jesus shall reign where're the sun does his successive journeys run,' seem curiously unprepared to accept that he might reign in some other way than as the Lord of your civilization. Your God has become too small, a mere civilizational idol, the largest tribal god history has yet witnessed, but a tribal god nonetheless.

"The crucial question for you is whether you can make the breakthrough, the critical breakthrough, to a new level of consciousness, a new level of universality, whether you can transcend the particularism to which you have, in your ethnocentrism, reverted and serve the one Lord, Jesus Christ, the Lord of history: 'He is Lord of all.' "

NOTE

1. *Mission Trends No. 1*, ed. Gerald H. Anderson and Thomas F. Stransky (New York: Paulist Press, and Grand Rapids: Eerdmans, 1974), pp. 81–86.

12

Translational Theology:

An Expression of Christian Faith in a Religiously Plural World

John Ross Carter

"Christian Faith in a Religiously Plural World" is, indeed, an engaging topic—one that will be with us for some time, as, perhaps, it should. Several questions tend to be raised in grappling with such a topic. What is faith? How might it be discerned? What is its source? In what sense do we say "Christian faith" or "Christian" faith? What does it mean to speak of a plural world and how so one that is religiously plural? Is there a place for Christian faith in a religiously plural world? Does a recognition that this world is religiously plural suggest a failure, in some sense, of Christian faith? Does the situation in which the Christian church finds itself today, one religious institution among others, engender fear and trembling within the Christian community or rekindle a resolve to convert humankind even at the risk of renewing an attitudinal orientation called by some "Christian triumphalism"?

Perhaps the easiest way to handle such questions might be to parry them or to ignore them and be lulled into a laissez-faire theological solipsism: each person to his or her own experiences, each tradition to its own perspectives. Or perhaps these questions might be postponed, relegated for the time being to a "back burner" consciousness, held there to be answered some time in the future, probably by someone else.

Christians have had faith sufficient to grapple with these or similar questions and, as the symposium at Washington and Lee has demonstrated, have had the resolve to do this publicly and formally, in a manner that sharply focuses before religion departments *and* the church the topic "Christian Faith in a Religiously Plural World."

Different theological positions have been presented by a number of theologians. Some have spoken of a discontinuity, of a tension, a "dynamic," a dialectic. Recurrent interpretive themes have been frequent: special and general revelation, particularism, the particularity of Christ or the Christian tradition, as well as universalism, the universal message of the Christian faith, the universal soteriological process that God has engendered in the hearts of all religious persons. In most instances, Protestant theologians have aspired to formulate a position that is biblically based, although interpretations of what "biblically based" means are not always in accord.

During the Washington and Lee symposium, a lacuna in the considerations became apparent: What is the role of Christian Scripture in a consideration of Christian faith within a religiously plural world?[1] Protestant theologians, especially in the context of religious pluralism, are met with the requirement of explicating the particularity of the Christ-event as God's saving activity to all religious persons *and* with the particularity of the Bible as the account of that saving activity. Some within the Christian community have attempted to develop a theological position from the Bible that would enable them to relate the Christian tradition to other traditions without theologically delimiting God's saving relationship with humankind and without being morally divisive between religious persons. Others within the Christian community have found in the Bible a charge to extend the Christian confession on this globe through conversion of the hearts and minds of all humankind and thereby to heal the cleavage between communities through discipleship under one Lord. There is a tension between these twin thrusts within the Christian tradition. This tension poses what Minor Rogers called a *kōan* for some and an unresolvable dilemma for other Christians. The situation in which Christians find themselves in a religiously plural world is one that demands of all prayerful reflection.

During an open discussion period following a presentation at the symposium, one featured speaker was asked whether his position was based on the Bible. Immediately the speaker replied, "I should hope so." Why, one might ask, was the reply given so readily? Why with such sober conviction? And, perhaps more germane to the concern here, why was the question raised in the first place? I should think it was, perhaps, a leading question designed either to establish a common premise or to terminate further discussion. Further, I should think the question and the response reflect a shared conviction that the task set for Christian theology in a religiously plural world must include a consideration of the significance of Scripture for the Christian tradition as it has developed and for Christian thought and practice today.

Wilfred Cantwell Smith, one of the speakers at the symposium, has written about the need to study the Bible in a relational and historical context: to study Scripture as a phenomenon manifestly significant in the religious life of humankind; to study the Bible as Scripture; to study how it arose, how it was adopted as Scripture, how people have approached it, what they have done with it and been enabled to do because of it through the centuries until today.[2] A subdivision implicit in Professor Smith's more general concern, although not explicitly addressed by him, would be the study of processes of translating the Bible, not only into western languages but also into other languages through which enormously influential religious apprehensions have been expressed for centuries by persons participating in the major religious traditions of Asia and elsewhere in the world. This would be a study not primarily of the dates and number of translations, but rather a study of attitudes toward the translating process itself, of theological issues raised in the translating process, and of ramifications of attitudes and issues in the history of humankind's religiousness and for Christian faith.

The history of Christian thought has been a history of communication and to no small extent has this history been one of translation, an activity of transferring concepts from one medium into another, the conveying of concepts from one language into another—a process, in the Christian context, having two inseparably intertwined strands: theology and language.

Donald Dawe noted one strand, the theological, when he said,

The "name of Jesus" is the disclosure of the pattern of God's action in human salvation. As such, it is open to translation. This "name" may be translated or given fresh expression in differing times and places. It is not in the continuity of a verbalism but in faithfulness to its meaning that the saving power revealed in Jesus is actualized. This is true because the "name of Jesus" is the disclosure of the structure of new being. . . . So the universality of Christianity is grounded in the translatability of the "name of Jesus," not in the imposition of particular formularies on others. This power of new being operates throughout the world under the names of many religious traditions. It is recognized and celebrated by Christians because they know its pattern or meaning through Jesus of Nazareth.

John Carman, in his consideration of the concept "religion," touched upon the twin strands in this process of translation.

The concept of religion goes back to western Christian translation language, and that, in turn, goes back to the Christian willingness to *translate* their sacred scriptures into other languages, perhaps derived from the Hellenistic Jews' decision to translate the Hebrew Bible into Greek. Their willingness to translate sacred words presupposes a confidence in a common element in human language and thus in human nature. A common element makes it possible for sacred truths to be expressed in another language. We are now so familiar with the process of translation as Christians that we may not understand how daring an undertaking was the Hellenistic Jews' translation of the Hebrew Bible, nor how important was their belief in the divine guidance of that translation. If we survey human religious practice, however, we see that translation or retranslation of sacred scriptures and liturgies has often been forbidden and very often, including in Christian circles, been viewed with deep suspicion.

I suggest that the human universal "religion" is by a circuitous route derived from early and later Christian confidence in the universal comprehensibility of the Christian message and the universal applicability of Christian piety. The divine Word can be expressed in differing human words because that divine Word is somehow behind every human being capable of uttering words.

Professor Dawe's notion of the "translatability of the 'name of Jesus' " and Professor Carman's affirmation that the "divine Word can be expressed in differing human words because that divine Word is somehow behind every human being capable of uttering words" suggest a translational theology.

Translational theology is the attempt to provide new form for traditional content, to give new expression to the salvific activity of God in Christ. The newness which translational theology seeks is not merely the novel. Rather, it is the fresh attempt to make relevant responses to the issues and questions raised by men and women within the Christian community *and* in other religious communities as they encounter one another in different times, in different places, and in different contexts.

Translational theology is immensely complex. The notion of "translatability of the 'name of Jesus' " pivots on one's apperception of the Christ-event and one's interpretations of the testimony of Scripture. An affirmation that "it is possible for sacred truths to be expressed in another language," that "the divine Word can be expressed in different human words," certainly represents the understanding endorsed by an impressive list of dedicated Christian biblical translators. But, in the process of translating, which human words in another language are to be used? Two levels of the process of translating sharply appear; on one level, a Christian translator might recognize the possibility "for sacred words to be expressed" through translation "in another language" and might discern that the "divine Word can be expressed" through translation "in different human words." Yet, on another level, a Christian translator might perceive sacred truths as having been already expressed and the divine Word already communicated through another language, in other religious traditions, in different human words.

Translational theology is *relational,* a sustained inquiry into the working of grammar and of God, an engaging study in matters of syntax and salvation, an investigation of possible connections between persons aspiring to live life religiously.

There is probably no occasion, in the process of developing an authentic self-understanding of Christian faith in a religiously plural world, on which the issue of particularity and universality within the Christian vision is more keenly sensed than in the activity of translating the Bible into languages that have played an enormous role in the world's major religious traditions and cultural complexes. Technical terms abound, technical in the sense that the terms are peculiarly related to particular religious orientations expressed through doctrinal apperceptions and communal affirmations. When might a proper occasion arise and what particular interpretation of God's revelatory activity in Christ would be requisite for one to draw upon a weighty concept in another religious tradition and set that down as an approximate translation for a central biblical concept? What is an appropriate balance between the Bible as scripture, as canon, and one's discernment of Jesus in light of Professor Dawe's comment, "In knowing Jesus, Christian faith is provided with the *canon*—the measuring stick—by which the activity of God may be discerned and confessed"? I do not wish to appear to be a biblicist tottering on the pinnacle of bibliolatry. Christians, gratefully, continue to stand in the wake of John when he courageously chose *logos* to represent the pre-existing Word of God that became "enfleshed." One wonders whether similar moves will be frequently met in the future of the Christian tradition or whether John's translational theology will largely remain a matter of the past.

In a brief paper dealing with issues involved in translating New Testament Greek terms into New Testaments in Sanskrit, Hindi, and Sinhala or Sinhalese ("Recent Issues in Biblical Interpretation: The New Testament in Asian Languages," prepared for a discussion group at the Washington and Lee Symposium), I introduced the subject by referring to the Septuagint. Professor Carman, in his address, also referred to this translation produced by Jewish scholars. This translation was a daring undertaking that was of considerable significance not only for Jews but also for Christians. It appears that Christians became aware of the legitimacy of the Septuagint and recognized in it a norm endorsed by Jewish scholars working in Alexandria—their predecessors by more than three centuries. This translation of the Hebrew Scripture into Greek by learned Jewish men greatly facilitated the Christian attempts to share their vision of the saving activity of God in Christ.

Certainly, Jews and Christians utilized the Septuagint in different ways and for different purposes. Nevertheless, quite early Christians were working with sacred writings *in translation*, writings that came to be discerned as Scripture, namely, the Old Testament. In the incipient stages of the Christian movement one catches a glimpse of something quite extraordinary that, until recently, has not frequently been repeated: A situation occurred in which persons in one religious community were significantly assisted by the translation of Scripture produced by persons in another religious community. Recently, this interpenetration of translational activity is becoming more noticeable. Some Hindus and Buddhists, for example, have been indebted to Christians who—working as Indologists, Buddhologists, linguists, historians—have edited and translated Hindu and Buddhist Scriptures. Persons in one community have been significantly assisted by the translation of Scripture produced by persons in another religious community.

Translational theology is, indeed, relational. I wonder whether soon there might come a day when Hindus, Buddhists, and Muslims would provide for Christians significant and meaningful translations of the Bible.[3]

Translational theology is relational and personal. It involves a continuing task to discover in oneself and in Scripture a process of thinking that represents a continuity within the Christian tradition and that is in accord with the deepest apprehensions of religious truth of men and women of other religious communities. No easy task, this! But wholesomely exhilarating, I should think, for Christians whose intellect is buttressed by the Holy Spirit.

In our lifetime, we are witnesses to a momentous event in

translational theology. Sinhalese Christians—who have been reared in a culture shaped by the Theravada Buddhist tradition—have a mother tongue that is heavily weighted with religious insights handed down in prose and poetry, subtle argument and song by Buddhist men and women for centuries in Sri Lanka. Yet they have chosen to take a concept from this context and to place it where John placed *logos* in his prologue.[4]

Some Sinhalese Christians, our brothers and sisters through discipleship in Christ, have listened carefully to the testimony of some Sinhalese Buddhists, our brothers and sisters through the teachings of Christ, and have drawn upon their own religious experience to discern the magnificence of a Theravada Buddhist concept, *dhamma/dharma*. (*Dhamma* is the Pali form of the word known to the Sinhalese through their Buddhist tradition, while *dharma* is the Sanskrit form of the term.) These Sinhalese Christians have grappled intellectually with the concept within the Buddhist religious heritage. They have struggled with the moral issues of possible divisive reactions within and between the Buddhist and Christian communities in Sri Lanka and, perhaps, elsewhere. Assuredly, they have prayed for guidance in this demonstration of faith expressed through translational theology.

I first learned of the possibility of this development during the three year period in which my wife and I lived in Sri Lanka, 1968–1971. I should note I was a bit disquieted by the prospects. My doctoral dissertation was on *dhamma* as a religious concept within the Theravada tradition, and I was persuaded that the Christian translators were misunderstanding what Buddhists were saying. I believed that they were not alert to the Buddhists affirmation that *dhamma*, on the highest level, transcends personalistic ascriptions. Further, to say that *dhamma* became "enfleshed" (as would be necessary in the translation of John 1:14) would tend to limit the notion for some, bringing it to a *lower* order of consideration.[5] However, making such a judgment about the meaning of *dhamma* depends on personal attitudes and intentions. Wrestling with this kind of an interpretation illustrated to me how personal translational theology can be.

Linguistic proficiency and historical competence assist persons in their attempts to provide new translations like this, but whether or not this translation will become widely accepted depends greatly upon what Christians do with it. Should the prevailing attitude be one of "one-upmanship" or competitiveness, if not confrontation, with Buddhists, the translation will foster a divisive tendency between communities. Nor will the translation be widely accepted in Sri Lanka—of course by this I mean accepted widely by Buddhists and Christians —Christians will have demonstrated that they see more in *dharma*-person *(dharmayānō)* than in Word-person *(vākyayānō)*. They will have extended the horizon of their vision of Christ and will have deepened the bases of their self-understanding in Christ through the notion of *dharma*-person. Buddhists will have found occasion to rest at ease knowing that Christians, in their different way, have also discerned the fundamental good news shared for centuries by Buddhists: *dhamma/dharma*, salvific truth, abides and it is not remote from persons.

We will see very possibly developments in the use of the term *dhamma* by Sinhalese Christian translators. Just as *logos*, as a term, can appear both in John 1:1 and in Acts 18:11, "And he settled down with them a year and a half teaching the word of God *(logos tou theou)* among them," implying both a person and a doctrine, so also could the term *dhamma/dharma* be used in a variety of settings.[6] Similarly other terms with weighty Christian meaning will percolate through the Sanskrit, Hindi, and Sinhalese languages, to mention but a few, the first two contributing to the Hindu tradition and the third to the Theravada Buddhist tradition. The Christian attempts to provide translations in East Asia will give rise to related theological issues of growing complexity.

Translational theology is relational because it deals with the relationship between, on the one hand, one's own experience in Christ, the witness of the Christian community, and the testimony of Scripture, and, on the other hand, the other religious traditions. Translational theology is personal because a humble attitude and a wholesome intention are crucial to probing, reflectively as a Christian, the thoughts and aspirations held most dearly by persons in other religious communities. Through this relational and personal activity one seeks to understand the religious insights of others in order to allow a two-way sharing. It makes the Christian affirmations more comprehensible to others, and enables Christians to discern more completely their life in Christ in a religiously plural world.

Whether or not *dharmayānō, dharma*-person, continues in the Sinhala New Testament as a profoundly engaging translation of "the Word" (*logos*) depends not only upon the insights the term might enable Sinhalese Christians to gain but to a considerable degree upon the response of Sinhalese Buddhists. Christians would be ill-prepared for the future were we to think of this as only an isolated matter for a relatively few people halfway around the world. We must be alert to the possibility that this example of translational interaction might play an important part in sharing faithfully the Christian testimony of the saving activity of God in Christ and simultaneously deepening Christian faith in a religiously plural world.

Translational theology, of course, is also concerned with translating for the Christian community today the sacred truths of old. It is concerned with translating sacred truths, communicated in one mode of discourse, into a mode more comprehensible for persons in a secularized western setting. But the Christian community is neither in isolation, nor is it limited to the West. And "modernization" implies a mode of communication for many persons in Asia that is considered to be "like the West" because it is stripped of its religious heritage. The translational problems posed by the rise of modern secularity may well appear in nonwestern lands in the not too distant future.

Translational theology is exploratory and explicatory. It reflects the faith to doubt and to make a commitment to Christ. It requires a confidence in God sufficient to sustain an open-ended investigation into the religious history of humankind. Drawing upon what has been remembered by the Christian tradition and working with what one knows has enabled one to have faith, translational theology has the potential to reach out, to explore, and to extend the periphery of the Christian vision of humankind's religiousness. In this way it will help to disentangle from the extrinsic underbrush of human foibles and make clear the communal testimony in tradition and in Scripture of the saving activity of Christ. In this process there is engendered a broadening perspective and a deepening understanding through faith of the centrality of Christ in Christian faith and in a religiously plural world.

The Washington and Lee symposium—the ten speakers, the other participants, and the conscientious organizers —began this gyroscopic rethinking of Christian self-understanding in our contemporary world and did so graciously. Much remains to be done and needs to be done with balance and perspective in a multidirectional and multidimensional way.

If financial exigence were of little moment one could readily envisage the form future symposia on the theme "Christian Faith in a Religiously Plural World" might take in order to go beyond the point to which the Washington and Lee symposium brought us: not a backstitching activity attempting to consolidate a consensus among Christians, but an undertaking by Christians and others to explore, to explicate, to discern relations, to check attitudes and review intent, to become personally engaged with the religious lives of persons in other religious communities, to translate sacred truths for Christians and for others. These are the present demanding challenges for Christian theology and a natural expression of Christian faith. This is the task for translational theology.

Should the symposia be in North America, five areas of scholarly competence and intellectual experience would need to be present:

1. Christian theologians from North America representing expertise in systematic theology, historical theology, and, perhaps, as some say, philosophical theology; they would be able to relate their probes to the intellectual spirit of the times and contemporary life situations of Christians in this culture;

2. Leading Christian representatives from Asia, Africa, and Latin America—ministers, teachers, and translators—who are living in a context largely shaped by one or more of the major religious traditions. They would be in position to share the

process of self-understanding developing within the Christian communities in the religiously plural settings of their parts of the world.

3. Christian biblical scholars who could assist in understanding the early Christian efforts to communicate the saving activity of God as well as their interpretation of the Bible as Scripture; they would come to grips for the first time, perhaps, with the history of these developments in the Christian tradition and their relevance for Christians and others in a religiously plural world;

4. Christian historians of religion, who have spent a number of years studying a religious tradition and community other than their own; they could contribute insights derived from their perspective of two religious traditions seen against the backdrop of humankind's complex religious history;

5. Representatives of the other major religious traditions, persons knowledgeable of the Christian ministry in Asia or exposed to the Christian tradition in the West; they would, by their presence, keep sharply focused for Christians the reality of religious pluralism, and by their active participation could provide a sympathetic view of the Christian tradition from the vantage point of a person living within another religious community; they could give a constructively critical view of our failures and could share with Christians perceptions of the religious life that would enable us to converse more congruously with others.

Conversation among persons of faith is an objective for Christians as they carry on the work of translational theology; the challenge is ours and the task awaits our doing it. Conversion and the transformation of human lives were never our doing, never directly caused by us, in the first place. That remains in the domain of God.

NOTES

1. On a generic level, one could, conceivably, organize a symposium on faith, rather than "Christian faith," in a religiously plural world with a series of seminar discussions on the significance of Scripture for religious persons in the major religious traditions of humankind.

2. Wilfred Cantwell Smith, "The Study of Religion and the Study of the Bible," *Journal of the American Academy of Religion* 39, no. 2 (June 1971): 131–40.

3. Futuristic considerations are tantalizing. What might be some ramifications within the Christian community, in A.D. 2176, if the most exact edition of the Greek New Testament were that compiled by Japanese Buddhists and if the most precise, erudite translation were that rendered by Japanese Buddhists in Japanese? Conceivably, Christian historians would turn to the Hindus and Buddhists in this our current century to be informed by their interpretations of and responses to western scholarship as it deals with their own religious traditions. More could be said, of course, but I leave this aside.

4. I refer to *Nava Givisuma, The Sinhala New Testament: A Common New Translation* (approved by the Bible Society and the Catholic Bishops' Conference in Sri Lanka), 1975. The first printing of this translation was in 1973, of 5,000 copies. The second printing, 1975, was of 3,000 copies. This translation is relational in an additional sense because of its ecumenical base within the Christian community in Sri Lanka. It is endorsed by both Protestants and Roman Catholics.

5. Strictly speaking, the recent Sinhalese translation does not convey the notion "enfleshed" held in the Greek at John 1:14 (*sarx egeneto*) but says "the *dharma*-person became a human being" (*dharmayānō minisatbava gena*) differing from Sinhalese translations of 1921 and 1931, "the Word-person became flesh" (*vākyayānō māmsavatva*).

6. *The Sinhala New Testament: A Common New Translation*, reading "word of God" (*deviyan vahansēgē vacanaya*) in Acts 18:11, might conceivably read in the future, "*dharma* of God" (*deviyan vahansēgē dharmaya*).

13

Is There a Theravada Buddhist Idea of Grace?

Mahinda Palihawadana

In March 1973, I read a paper before the Association of Asian Studies in Chicago entitled "Is There a Theravada Notion Comparable with Grace?" The paper was not published, because I felt that the inquiry was not complete and that I should reflect more on the issues that I raised, which were not only important doctrinally, but also were likely to affect Buddhist sensibility on several vital points. I realized that what I say on the subject will be said in vain, if it is, even formally let alone substantially, not in consonance with the basic "idiom" of the Buddhists. On a number of points, partly phraseological, my Chicago paper did not fulfill this requirement.

The notion that I took up for discussion was the Theravada notion of spiritual change indicated as *magga-dassana* (or simply *magga,* which normally means "path," as the "noble eightfold path" of conduct; it can also mean a moment of spiritual change).[1] Three years of further thinking on the matter makes me feel that it was a mistake to call it a notion "comparable" with *grace.*

This is not to say that I was entirely on the wrong track, or that my effort was unproductive. The evidence that I had gathered, I now think, allows me to say the following: "Behind the Buddhist notion of *magga* there is a recognition of certain basic issues. *Magga* expresses the Buddhist response to those issues. The same religious issues appeared to Christians and their response to them is the notion of grace." It does not allow me to say that *magga* and *grace* are "comparable"—which was a possible implication of what I then said. And yet the thrust of what I wanted to say was that behind both notions there seem to lie some nonsectarian truths—something that deserves our attention as a basic human issue, which both Buddhists and Christians have approached from their respective specific standpoints.

I

The basis of the Theravada notion of *magga* is the Buddhist view of the common state of human beings and their movement from that state into the liberated *(vimutta)* state. To the Theravadins it appeared that people in their common state were "defiled," "fettered," or "screened" with a variety of "obstacles" of the mind that made them self-centered and unfree.[2] To move away from this burdened and self-centered state was the main purpose of the religious life. This transformation takes place via a gnosis, via "self"-knowledge: So the movement is also one from "delusion" to wisdom.[3]

Just as the Christians, viewing human beings as being in sin or in a state of corrupted nature, considered that it was not possible for them in that condition to do good or to love or to be redeemed,[4] the Theravadins also acknowledged that the question of how to leave delusion was an issue to be faced. A late canonical text states the problem thus:

If he rejects past corruptions then he extinguishes what has been extinguished, stops what has ceased, dispatches what has already gone away, puts an end to what has passed away, rejects the past which does not exist. . . . If he rejects future corruptions, then he rejects what has not been born, . . . what has not arisen, . . . what has not appeared, rejects the future which does not exist. . . . If he rejects present corruptions, then the lustful rejects lust, the hateful hate, . . . the deluded delusions (*Patisambhidāmagga*, II, 217).[5]

Thus the issue that we are referring to, viz., how the defiled could ever become undefiled, was one to which the teachers of Theravada were alive, at least from as far back as the third century B.C., when the Abhidhamma texts took final shape. It was still recognized as an issue eight centuries or so afterwards, as we can see from what the fifth-century commentator Buddhaghosa says:

Does [the mind as the *magga* occasions] discard these factors [of defilement] as [remains] of the past or as [potentialities] of the future, or as [existent factors] of the present? If the first two be the case, the effort would turn out to be in vain, because what are to be discarded do not exist [as present factors, hence not available to be operated upon]. If the third be the case, the effort would be equally fruitless, because then effort and what it seeks to do away with would be co-existing [and hence] the development of *magga* would be tinged with the defiled conditions [of the mind]; or [we would then have to assume] that the defilements [and consciousness] exist in a state of [mutual] dissociation (*Visuddhimagga*, XXII, 78).

Stated this way, the problem seems to be more intricate in a nontheistic context than in a theistic one. How did the Buddhists proceed to answer it in the context of their nontheistic approach?

The Theravada teachers who posed this problem might have seen a hint of the answer to it in a notion which already the Buddha seems to have adumbrated:

Monks, for a person who is virtuous, well-endowed with virtue, there is no need of the effort of will: "Let freedom from remorse arise in me." It is a matter of nature that freedom from remorse arises in such a person.

The passage goes on in the same strain to indicate that

when one is in delight, joy arises as a matter of nature;
when one is joyful, physical relaxation arises as a matter of nature;
when one is physically relaxed, happiness arises as a matter of nature;
when one is happy, integration of mind[6] arises as a matter of nature;
when one is of integrated mind, there arises the seeing and knowing
    of things as they are, as a matter of nature;

when one sees and knows things as they are, the realization of "the
wisdom-vision" of deliverance arises as a matter of nature.
In this way, spiritual states themselves make spiritual states to flow
in;[7] spiritual states themselves make spiritual states to come to fulfil-
ment, for the passage from this shore to the other shore. (*Anguttara
Nikāya,* Dasaka Nipāta, II)[8]

What was rendered in the text as "effort of will" is well
explained in the commentary. According to it, effort of will
(*cetānaya karanīyam*) is "that which is to be done after, or
with, deliberate thought."[9] The definition of *cetanā* in
the *Visuddhimagga* associates it with not only purposeful
"thought," but also with striving (*āyūhana*), making arrange-
ment (*samvidahana*) and effort (*ussāha*).[10] The intention of the
original statement is perfectly clear: No fuss on your part, no
process of setting up a goal and striving toward it, can bring on
the next development. It comes naturally when the right conditions have appeared.

It is fascinating to note how this ancient statement explains
the continuous movement through all the "steps" of the salvific process as a matter of natural development. The whole
notion is rooted in the nontheistic, impersonalist approach
that is the essential flavor of the tradition of the early Buddhists. This extremely interesting passage is one on which we
should ponder more and more.

Although the Buddha is shown here to be trusting to a
natural development all the way as far as the supreme inner
change, it would not be consistent with the spirit of the Buddhist teaching to say that one had only to be "virtuous" and all
the rest would naturally follow. Further, if that was the intention of this passage, the step by step description would also be
quite uncalled for.

What seems to be legitimate to infer from this passage is that
at each step there is a participatory role for the "seeker" and
then a natural development that occurs without the seeker
making an effort in that direction. Thus,

being virtuous,
one naturally becomes capable of being without remorse,

being free from remorse,
one naturally becomes capable of experiencing delight

and so on.

So, three things seem to be here implied: (1) The concerned ones participate; it is not that they do nothing. (2) But they do not "dictate" to the process of change. (3) The change occurs as a matter of "unwilled evolution," under circumstances appropriate for such evolution, one of which is right participation.

The "meditation" ("seeing what is," etc.) then is not the enforcing of a change that one has, while still being "defiled," assumed to be the right thing for oneself. It is rather a step to allow the circumstances to develop in which the right natural change "flows in."

II

As far as the notion of grace is concerned, our attempt here can be no more than to locate the central issue behind its many dimensions and formulations. This in itself cannot be an easy task and one is bound to oversimplify complex issues, however earnestly one may wish not to offend.

The central issue seems to us to be the realization that human beings are in a state of spiritual weakness and are not able to take a leap out of this "in order to be healed and . . . in order to carry out works of supernatural virtue."[11] But in point of historical fact, people have indeed taken that leap. The grace notion gives a theistic explanation of this experience.

In the context of a discussion of the Buddhist interpretation of this phenomenon, what seems to be relevant in the theistic viewpoint, such as that of the Christians, are the following:

a. The actual recognition of spiritual change, from weakness to strength, from sin to blessedness.
b. The notion of people's inability to effect this change by any acts of the will.
c. The active agent in the change being regarded as God, moved by love.
d. The idea that human beings nevertheless have a role to

play. (This is a factor in St. Thomas Aquinas and St. Augustine on grace. "It is the part of man to prepare his soul. . . . And yet he does not do this without the help of God moving him . . . ").[12]

We cannot hope to find *c.* in the Buddhist experience and *d.* will also significantly differ in any Buddhist explanation of the matter. Vast as are these differences, the few points of agreement do not appear to be negligible, and they encourage us to continue the inquiry, particularly in order to clarify the Theravada interpretation of what the Christians see as a loving act of God.

III

The Buddhist canonical text *Anguttara Nikāya* is a very important tract in the doctrinal and scriptural history of the Theravada Buddhists. The salvific process that is implied by it must have been the subject of devoted study by the doctors of the Buddhist Sangha (community of monks) over the centuries. The content of that study has been recorded for posterity in several forms, of which by far the most comprehensive is the *Visuddhimagga* ("Path of Purity") of Buddhaghosa, the famous fifth-century commentator.

Let us follow the Theravada "pilgrim" on this three-laned path—not all the way, but at those important points where we need to see him, as portrayed by Buddhaghosa.

Buddhaghosa's pilgrim may perhaps be an increasingly scarce entity at this point in the history of the Theravada faith. Some may even doubt if human beings ever will strictly adhere to a path such as the one he outlines. Neither of these facts, however, can minimize the historical value of his discussion and the illumination that it throws on much that concerns the thought of the Theravadins.

The first point that one would like to emphasize about Buddhaghosa's path of purity is that it consists of a part that can be described as the field of possible action and a part to which that description would not be applicable. Let us take up this point.

The three-fold salvific process, which by another metaphor Buddhaghosa likens to a tree, has the two roots of *sīla* and *samādhi*. The first is virtuous or moral conduct, for which Buddhaghosa recommends a strenuous discipline, and the second is what is said to lead to integration of mind.

The third aspect of the path is what by the other metaphor constitutes the trunk of the tree. This is *pannā* (Sanskrit *prajnā*), which means wisdom, insight, or realization—which gives a profound understanding as opposed to perceptual or intellectual knowledge.

True to his style, Buddhaghosa gives many classifications of *pannā*, most of which are of no interest to us. But one distinction he consistently makes is crucial to the understanding of the teaching of the *Visuddhimagga*, and indeed of the entire Theravada system of thought. It is a basic qualitative distinction according to which there is one kind of *pannā* that is concerned with the understanding of the nature of mind and its defilements, of human beings as they are. Buddhaghosa calls this the *pannā* that is concerned with the mundane (*lokiya*). In sharp contrast to this stands the other kind of *pannā*, which gives a vision of that which is beyond the mundane (*lokuttara*). [13]

This vital distinction should in no way be ignored. The only proper way to take this distinction into account is to say that the Theravada salvific process has in reality four aspects rather than three, viz.

1. *sīla*
2. *samādhi*
3. *lokiya pannā*
4. *lokuttara pannā*

The Theravada realm of possible action is constituted by 1, 2, and 3 above. The fourth is outside that realm.

When we examine carefully what Buddhaghosa says under *pannā*, we see how only a part of it belongs to the sphere of "what one can do." Thus the first four chapters of his section on *pannā* (chaps. 14–17) are a description of doctrines, topic by topic. For Buddhaghosa this is the ground (*bhūmi*) on which the tree of wisdom is to grow. It is obvious from this treatment that the tradition regarded a doctrinal study to be the essential first steps in the field of *pannā*.

Chapters 18–20 of the *Visuddhimagga* are also doctrinal discussions, but with a more immediate aim: to render the understanding of the first three Truths more definitive and also to ascertain more deeply the particular characteristics of the Buddhist teachings on the psycho-physical personality. This section has a "more immediate aim" because its purpose is to help the pilgrim understand the nature of the mind's defilement. In chapter 20, the pilgrim is represented as trying to understand these teachings at a still more personal level by meditative introspection *(vipassanā)*.

A very important aspect of the discussion is that concerning the *sankhārās*: [14] the ground-elements of the psyche that are in a state of constant flux. These processes arise and vanish, but as they vanish, they become the ground for the arising of similar new processes. This proclivity of theirs creates the continuous movement of psychical phenomena. It is in this movement that the mind's defilements (which themselves are *sankhārās)* renew themselves without cessation. But no one can arrest the procession of the *sankhārās* by a forcible effort of will:

No one whosoever can say: "Let not the emerged *sankhārās* stabilize; let those stabilized not come to decline; let those that have declined not break up," and have a sway over them in any of these conditions *(Visuddhimagga,* XX, 47).

Study and meditation *(vipassanā)* are for bringing about a deep comprehension of all these processes. What was expected to occur in meditation can perhaps be gauged from the following:

The removal of the fetters of clinging-to-concepts . . . and conceit does not come about when there is the thought: "It is I who observe, it is *my* introspection."

The *sankhārās* themselves see the *sankhārās*, contemplate, discern, comprehend *(Visuddhimagga,* XX, 83).

This shows that the basis of meditation is the ability of the psychical processes to become self-aware, without the intrusion of a subject-object dichotomy (without a division into the seer and the seen, the "I" and the "mine"). And yet, meditation is an event in the field of psychical processes; it is not a stepping out of that field.

The comprehension at first hand through meditative introspection brings on a disenchantment;[15] and with disenchantment there springs up a spontaneous new decision:

> The cause for the [continued] birth of defilements is the [proclivity of psychical processes] to arise [from the ground of evanescing processes]. Seeing the ill-effects of this, the mind takes to non-arising (*Patisambhidāmagga* II, 218).

One may wonder: "Is this not also the activity of the mind?" The phrasing suggests the attitude of creative experiment appearing in a flash before the mind's eye: "Let me be quiet, wholly relaxed." There is a world of difference between this and the deliberate, future-oriented, striving (*āyūhana*) aspect of the *sankhārās*—a difference to be understood by personal experience rather than by theoretical reasoning. This reminds us of a still earlier canonical passage in a similar context:

> There as he stood at the most refined state of perception, this thought would occur to him: "The worse it is for me when I activate mental processes, the better when I do not. If I exercise mental processes and will, these perceptions would cease and other gross perceptions would arise." And as he exercises neither mental processes nor will, that [refined] perception itself ceases and other gross perceptions do not arise (*Digha Nikāya*, I, 184–85).[16]

These developments did not have a negative significance in the eyes of the Theravadins. The positive note is struck by Buddhaghosa when he says that, along with these developments,

> there arises strong faith-resolve, energy becomes firmly set, awareness well-established, mind well-collected . . . and the conviction arises: "Now *magga* will come into being! " (*Visuddhimagga*, XXI, 128–29).

Earlier texts characterize this strong positive element as "the faculty [of being able to know] that what was [hitherto] not realized will be realized."

The traditional sentiments associated with this state, called the *anannātan-nassāmītindriya,* are well rendered in the following words of Mrs. C.A.F. Rhys Davids: "The inspiring sense of assurance that dawns upon the earnest student that he will come to know the Ambrosial Way unknown in wordly pursuits. . . . As one coming to a dwelling out of his usual beat and receiving garland and raiment and food, realizes that he is encountering new experiences."[17]

This is the end of our pilgrim's operations in the field of possible action. What follows, the "Purity-of-wisdom Vision" does not belong to this field, as is sharply thrown into relief by some of Buddhaghosa's own words in relation to this point:

Now there is *nothing more to be done* by the one who wishes to provide himself with the insight of the first *magga.* What could have been done has already been done by him (*Visuddhimagga,* XXII, 3).

One must emphasize the fact that this assertion that mind has come to the end of the field of possible action is made even before the first of the "defilements" has been destroyed.

The "creative passivity" at the end of the field of possible action serves as the ground for the emergence of salvific change:

Thus, as the grosser darkness which enveloped truth disappeared in him, his mind no longer takes to any of the psychical processes at all. . . . Whatever serves as the occasion for psychical processes, whatever activates them—all that appears to him as hindrances. . . .

Then, there emerges [in him] that [flash of] insight . . . which turns in the direction of Nibbāna and which, rising above the ordinary ground of the mundane, . . . enrolls him in the New Lineage. . . . [18]

This insight [arises and] subsides, as if signalling to *magga:*"Now, be born!" and *magga* too, as if not failing the given signal, follows on that flash of insight and arises, penetrating and breaking through the mass of greed and illwill and delusion that hitherto was unpierced. . . .

This *magga* not only breaks through the mass of greed and ill will . . . but also dries up the ocean of ill in the round of existences, . . . brings the seven noble treasures into one's presence, . . . quietens all enmities and fears, leads one to the cherished sonship of the supremely perfect Buddha and conduces to the attainment of hundreds of other advantages (*Visuddhimagga*, XXII; from paragraphs 4, 5, 11, and 14).[19]

Thus the *magga* event, swiftly arising after a moment of the mind's creative passiveness, regenerates and makes a new person of the pilgrim and gives him his first vision of Nibbāna. It is the true blessed event of the religious life of the Theravada Buddhist. What is infused into mind at that moment is *lokuttara pannā:* "world-transcending insight." At that moment he moves out of the third phase and into the fourth or the salvific path briefly described above.

At this salvific moment, Nibbāna (the ultimate state of salvation), which was hitherto extraneous to experience, becomes involved with it as a "present factor"—not in the sense that Nibbāna makes itself manifest or becomes an active factor in any way, but in the sense that the mind as it is at this moment has become capable of "seeing Nibbāna."[20] And the significant thing is that it is only when Nibbāna became a present factor that the defilements were affected; nothing could touch them until then, however arduous the meditations. It is in this way that Theravadins can understand the canonical saying, "Were (the Unborn) not there, there would be no final transcendence for the one that is born" (Udāna 80-81). As the *Visuddhimagga* puts it:

Magga . . . conquers defilements by means of the goodly vision which is conjoint with it   and Nibbāna conquers defilements by means of the goodly vision of which it is the object (*Visuddhimagga*, VII, 78).[21]

In other words, Nibbāna "conquers" human weaknesses via the vision in which it is the object and that vision is part and parcel of the *magga*-event.

IV

To sum up, the Theravada notion of spiritual change signifies the following:

a. An ordering of life and dedicated study and meditation initiate the process.

b. In the course of this, one sees the nature of the proclivities of the psychical processes; they then cease and the mind becomes spontaneously passive and relaxed.

c. At this point, the transforming vision of insight occurs and the defilements become destroyed.

d. Nibbāna is the indispensable "present factor" in this event.

And, of course, this is a blessed event by any reckoning: To the Theravadins it is *the* event of supreme spiritual distinction. Through it alone one moves away from self-centeredness.

We might also sum up these facts in another way.

a. The operation of the law of "causal orderliness"[22] (in its positive aspect and in its negative aspect) explains the events in the Buddhist salvific process: (i) "something done," etc., followed by "natural changes"; (ii) "absence of conditions" followed by "absence of consequences."

b. The final element in this procession of events is the brief cessation of *sankhāra* activity. This last event contains a new element: non-operation of will, of the "wanting-to-become-something." This amounts to the "absence of the conditions for defilement."[23]

c. In the next events, there is the "discarding of defilement," which happens because the other factor necessary for it now takes place, namely, contact with the "reality-beyond-the-world" *(lokuttara dhamma)*. But this contact is "not a production in one's being, but an encounter at first hand."[24]

What then is *magga* in the final analysis?

It is the natural occurrence of a mental event, at a moment of total relaxation of the usual psychical activities, which, (1) discards vitiating psychic characteristics; (2) provides first-hand acquaintance with transcendent reality; and (3) gives profound understanding of truth.[25]

It is therefore the spontaneous generation of a qualitative newness of being, a true psychical *mutation* which raises one from one's weaknesses and brings on a total change. Theravada holds that newness of being occurs any way at all times: "All elements of being come into existence . . . having been previously non-existent."[26] "[All] states, not having arisen before, . . .arise now."[27] The difference at the *magga* event is, inter alia, that in it there is the annulment of the vitiating ground of defilement, whence the newness here is qualitative."[28]

Increasingly it is becoming clear that the ground covered by the theistic religions' concept of God is, in the Buddhist tradition, covered not by a single concept, but by two, viz., (1) the uncaused ultimate reality, and (2) the actively operating, self-sustaining cosmic law of causation. Effort and all that pertains to the active religious life is in the realm of (2). It performs its due functions and ends when its own limitations are understood. It is at this end of the *lokiya* religious sphere that the liberating contact with (1) is made. Obviously, this liberating event is possible because (1) is an ever-present factor, although it is itself not envisaged as an "actor" participating in the event.

Does this account of the notion of *magga* conflict with the widely-held view that liberation according to Theravada is something to be obtained by intense personal effort? The purpose of this paper is in part to show that that view could be misleading unless it is also understood that personal effort is only the "setting" for the realization of the highest religious truth, that the highest realization can take place only when effort ceases to be, having exhausted its scope and having brought about the knowledge that it too is a barrier to be broken down.[29]

The necessity of this corrective becomes obvious when we ponder the implications of such a statement as Buddhaghosa's on realization ("realized realities are those that are attained to without having been produced in one's being")[30] and the significance of *anatta* ("no self"): The supreme truth to be realized is not a product of "my" efforts, not a conceptual entity to be visualized or concocted by my mind.

The difference between the theistic approach and the

Buddhist one has not been ignored in this study. In fact, it is a study of comparable issues and contrasting responses. Pursuing our study within these limits, however, it was possible to see the elements of a common religious conviction: The redeeming change in a person takes place not ultimately by exercising the will, but at its cessation, which is an indispensable factor for contact with supreme reality; it is this contact that truly renews and transforms the person.

NOTES

1. *Magga* normally means "path" as in the compound *magga-phala.* There are two technical meanings attached to the word: (1) in *ariya atthangika magga* it means (the noble eightfold) path, as a course of conduct. (2) In the other usage (either as *ariya magga* or simply as *magga*), it means the moment of spiritual change as well as that event and the content of mind at that moment.

2. "Defilements," etc., are enumerated and described in *Visuddhimagga of Buddhaghosacariya,* ed. H. C. Warren, Harvard Oriental Series, Vol. 41 (Cambridge: Harvard University Press, 1950), XXII, 47–63.

3. That is, from *moha* to *pannā.* The former is perhaps better rendered as "unawareness."

4. A. C. Pegis, *Introduction to St. Thomas Aquinas* (New York: Modern Library, 1948), p. 655.

5. *Patisambhidāmagga,* ed. A. C. Taylor (London: H. Froude, Pali Text Society, 1905–07), II, 217.

6. *Samādhi* is usually translated as "concentration." Since the word *(samtāt /dhā)* etymologically means "the being collected (or held) together," I prefer to render it as "integration."

7. *Abhisandeti* is from root *sa(n)d-,* "to flow" (Sanskrit, *syand-).* The causative *sandeti* means "causes to flow."

8. *Anguttara Nikāya,* ed. E. Hardy (London, Luzac & Co., Pali Text Society, 1958), Part V, II.

9. *Cetetvā kappetvā pakappetvā kātabban. Manorathapuranī, Commentary on the Anguttava Nikāya,* ed., Hermann Kopp (London: Oxford University Press, Pali Text Society, 1956), part V, p. 1.

10. *Visuddhimagga,* XIV, 135.

11. Pegis, *Introduction to St. Thomas Aquinas,* p. 655.

12. Ibid., p. 663. Cf. Charles Journet, *The Meaning of Grace* (New York: P. J. Kenedy, 1960), pp. 21, 26.

13. *Visuddhimagga,* XIV, 9, *lokiya* and *lokuttara.* The same distinction as *dhamma-tthiti-nāna* and *nibbāne nāna* or as *ācayagāmi* and *apacayagāmi.*

14. *Sankhārā* has a wide range of meanings. *Visuddhimagga* (XVII, 45–46) notes the best known four: (1) all conditioned phenomena, (2) material and

immaterial phenomena resulting from past action, (3) morally beneficial and morally vitiative volitional processes, (4) physical and psychical momentum.

15. Called *ādīnava-, nibbidā-,* and *muncitukāmyatā.*

16. *Anguttara Nikaya, Dasaka Nipata,* I, 184–85.

17. Mrs. C.A.F. Rhys Davids, *A Buddhist Manual of Psychological Ethics* (London: Royal Asiatic Society, 1900), p. 86.

18. "The insight . . . which . . . enrolls him in the New Lineage": The Pali term for this is *gotrabhū-nāna. Visuddhimagga,* XXII, 5, defines this as that "which passes beyond the kinship of average men . . . [and] enters into the kinship of Ariyas" (*ariya:* noble/aristocratic).

19. Abridged quotation. For a translation of the whole see P. Maung Tin, ed., *The Path of Purity, Being a Translation of Buddhaghosa's Visuddhimagga* (London: Oxford University Press, Pali Text Society, 1923–31), pp. 824ff.

20. *Visuddhimagga,* XXII, 127, says that the *sacchikiriyā* function of *magga* amounts to "encounter with the supra-mundane," being (a) contact through primary vision (*dassana*) at the first *magga* and (b) contact by way of enlargement or development (of the primary vision) at the susequent *maggas; Visuddhimagga,* XXII, 125–26, explain *sacchikiriyā* as *phassanā:* contact. The first *magga* is called *dassana* (vision) because at it Nibbāna is first sighted.

21. *Visuddhimagga,* VII, 78, commenting on *sanditthi.*

22. *Idappaccayatā.* The usual formula is somewhat as follows: (a) "when this is there, that arises" and conversely (b) "when this is not there, that does not arise."

23. *Visuddhimagga,* XXII, 79.

24. *Visuddhimagga,* XXII, 126. This is an important definition which shows that Theravadins took Nibbāna definitely as a reality not of the mind, but one reachable by the mind (Cf. XVI, 71).

25. *Visuddhimagga,* XXII, 92, refers to four "functions" of *magga: Parinnā, pahāna, sacchikiriyā,* and *bhāvanā:* comprehension of the truths; discarding defilements; encountering Nibbāna, and deepening of that encounter.

26. *Visuddhimagga,* XX, 96.

27. *Visuddhimagga,* XX, 104.

28. *The Atthasalini, Buddhaghosa's Commentary on the Dhammasangani,* ed. Edward Mueller (London: H. Froude, Pali Text Society, 1897), p. 217: "Awakens and arises from the slumber of the continuum of defilement"; p. 214: "*Magga,* though world-transcending, arises, unlike Nibbāna." Rhys Davids, *Buddhist Manual,* p. 995: It is "neither corrupt nor baneful."

29. *The Atthasalini,* p. 214, describes the two spheres of the religious life as like building a brick wall and tearing it down, brick by brick.

30. *Visuddhimagga,* XXII, 126 states: "though not produced in one's continuum, those states which are known by knowledge entirely independent of another" as a description of "realized realities." The relevant Pali text is *attano santāne anuptadetvā pi ye dhammā kevalam aparapaccayena nānena nātā).*

Other Orbis Titles

GOD, WHERE ARE YOU?

by Carlos Mesters

Meditations and reflections on significant figures and events in the Bible. "We shall," says Mesters, "try to restore to the word of God the function that it ought to have: to serve as a light on the pathway of life, as a help to our own understanding of present-day reality in all its complexity."

ISBN 0-88344-162-4 CIP   *Cloth $6.95*

THE EXPERIENCE OF GOD

by Charles Magsam

"His range is comprehensive; his orientation is personal, biblical, communitarian; his tone is positive and encouraging: all in all, a one-volume course on how to be free wholesomely for God, for oneself and for others." *Prairie Messenger*

ISBN 0-88344-123-3   *Cloth $7.95*

ISBN 0-88344-124-1   *Paper $4.95*

JESUS OF NAZARETH

Meditations on His Humanity

by Jose Comblin

"St. Teresa of Avila warned her nuns to beware of any kind of prayer that would seek to eliminate all reference to the human aspect of Christ. I think Jose Comblin would agree that her warning also describes the theme of his extremely valuable book that can be read and re-read many times with great benefit." *Priests USA*

ISBN 0-88344-231-0   *Cloth $5.95*

PRAYER AT THE HEART OF LIFE

by Brother Pierre-Yves Emery

"Emery's approach is both realistic and down-to-earth and profound and moving. This book can be recommended to anyone interested in a practical analysis of prayer, particularly the specific relationship between prayer and life itself." *Review for Religious*

ISBN 0-88344-393-7   *Cloth $4.95*

PILGRIMAGE TO NOW/HERE

by Frederick Franck

"Every now and then a true gem of a book appears that fails to get caught up in the tide of promotion, reviews, and sales, and, despite its considerable merits, seems to disappear. Such a book is Dr. Frederick Franck's *Pilgrimage to Now/Here*. His *Zen of Seeing* has been a steady seller, and *The Book of Angelus Silesius* is moving well. What happened to *Pilgrimage*, which in many ways is a more important book? Since Orbis is known as a religious publishing house, many distributors and booksellers are reluctant to stock it. Yet this is a religious book in the most significant sense of that word—in what Frederick Franck would call the search for meaning—for it is an account of a modern pilgrimage by jet, bus, train, and on foot to visit holy places and meet Buddhist leaders and Zen masters in India, Ceylon, Hong Kong and Japan."

East West Journal

ISBN 0-88344-387-2   *Illustrated Paper $3.95*

BIBLICAL REVELATION AND AFRICAN BELIEFS

edited by Kwesi Dickson and Paul Ellingworth

"Essays by scholars who are themselves both African and Christian and who share a concern that Christian theology and African thought be related to each other in a responsible and creative way. There is no comparable book; this one should be in any library attempting serious coverage of either African thought or Christian theology." *Choice*

ISBN 0-88344-033-4   *Cloth $5.95*

ISBN 0-88344-034-2   *Paper $3.45*

IN SEARCH OF THE BEYOND

by Carlo Carretto

"The book describes an 'aloneness' that draws hearts closer together, a 'withdrawal' that enriches family and community ties, a love of God that deepens human love." *America*

ISBN 0-88344-208-6   *Cloth $5.95*

LETTERS FROM THE DESERT

by Carlo Carretto

"It has been translated into Spanish, French, German, Portuguese, Arabic, Japanese, Czech, and now, gracefully enough (from Italian) into English. I hope it goes into twenty-four more editions. It breathes with life, with fresh insights, with wisdom, with love." *The Thomist*

ISBN 0-88344-279-5   *Cloth $4.95*

THE GOD WHO COMES

by Carlo Carretto

"This is a meaty book which supplies on every page matter for reflection and a spur to the laggard or wayward spirit. It offers true Christian perspective." *Our Sunday Visitor*

ISBN 0-88344-161-0   *Cloth $4.95*

FREEDOM TO BE FREE

By Arturo Paoli

"Full of eye-opening reflections on how Jesus liberated man through poverty, the Cross, the Eucharist and prayer." *America*

ISBN 0-88344-143-8   *Paper $4.95*

SILENT PILGRIMAGE TO GOD

The Spirituality of Charles de Foucauld

by a Little Brother of Jesus
preface by Rene Voillaume

"Sets out the main lines of Charles de Foucauld's spirituality and offers selections from his writings." *America*

ISBN 0-88344-459-3   *Cloth $4.95*

AFRICAN TRADITIONAL RELIGION: A DEFINITION

by E. Bolaji Idowu

"This important book is the first to place the study of African religion in the larger context of religious studies. . . . It includes an index and notes. There is no comparable work; this one should be in any collection on African religion." *Choice*

ISBN 0-88344-005-9   *Cloth $6.95*

THE PATRIOT'S BIBLE

edited by John Eagleson and Philip Scharper

"Following the terms of the Declaration of Independence and the U.S. Constitution, this faithful paperback relates quotes from the Bible and from past and present Americans 'to advance the kingdom and further our unfinished revolution.' " *A.D.*

ISBN 0-88344-377-5   *Paper $3.95*

THE RADICAL BIBLE

adapted by John Eagleson and Philip Scharper

"I know no book of meditations I could recommend with more confidence to learned and unlearned alike." *St. Anthony Messenger*

ISBN 0-88344-425-9   *Cloth $3.95*
ISBN 0-88344-426-7   *Pocketsize, paper $1.95*

UGANDA: THE ASIAN EXILES

by Thomas and Margaret B. Melady

"Takes its inspiration from the announcement in August 1972 by General Idi Amin Dada, President of Uganda, that he was told in a dream to order the expulsion of all Asians from Uganda. Tom and Margaret Melady were there and were witness to the tragic events. The book surveys the gruesome events following the expulsion order and the irrational pattern of Amin's record as well as providing a factual background of the Asian presence in Africa. The historical, economic and social complexity of the African-Asian-European situation in Uganda is made clear. Stories of personal devotion and heroism put flesh on the facts." *Religious Media Today*

ISBN 0-88344-506-9 CIP   *Cloth $6.95*